Strangely

A Collection of Poems About People Who Are Different

by

John Hilton

©2019 John Hilton

Cover painting ('Lady') and book design by John Hilton.

Also available in paperback and Kindle

poetry
Words on Paper
Poems (1993-2016)
The Silence of a Written Word
Narrator as Witness: **Narrative Poems**
The Act of Feeling: **Selected Poems**
Words for the Passing of Time*

prose fiction
That is the Question [novel]
Tales [stories]
More Tales [stories]
Fresh Tales [stories]*

plus
Trust and Love [essays & prayers]
The Stars and I [SF writings]

*In preparation

Introduction

Thank you for taking the time to look at this introduction. Strange People is not a collection of new poems.

Instead this book represents a combination and expansion of three titles I published on the Kindle platform. **Cracked** is a collection of poems subtitled "A collection of poems about people who are mad and people who are sad". As the subtitle suggests, the poems centre around issues such as mental health, trauma and similar tales of damaged psyche. **Tales of People** bore the subtitle "poems about imagined lives." That volume contained examples of invented characters and how they react to the fictional situations in which I place them. **All This Expression** is subtitled "a collection of poems about art and artists" and does pretty much what it says. Inevitably there is a large amount of thematic overlap between the volumes, particularly the first two. All three of these collections were published in 2014 and are fairly slim volumes. None of them were considered for publication in book form.

However, I always had a soft spot for them and recently began to wonder if there was a way to bring them out in paper form. This omnibus edition is the result of that desire.

Since the original volumes were centred around the theme of people whose lives would most likely be considered to be neither typical nor normal by most people, I thought that **Strange People** was an apt title for the combined collection. I also decided that I would keep the original orders of contents from Kindle the volumes intact. Therefore the sequence of poems that runs from **Man in the Corner** to **Like a Sun Rising** represent a reprint of **Cracked,** the sequence from **The Sound of Blue** to **Closer** is from **Tales of People** and the sequence from **And She Sings** through to **Song to Bob** is **All This Expression**.

Between those sequences I have inserted five newer poems that were written after the three Kindle books had been published. **Anaesthesia** first appeared in the book **The Silence of the Written Word** and **Razor Blades and Other Pain Killers** first appeared in **Words on Paper**. The poems **A Midnight Quiet** and **Song From the Edge of Forever** come from the collection **Words From the Passing of Time** which has not yet been published, so you could view it as an exclusive preview. The last poem in the book is also an addition. **Thespian** comes from **The Silence of the Written Word** and closes this volume as I felt it combines the various themes that gave the original volumes their particular flavour rather neatly and seems an ideal way to both sum up and bring to a close this new volume.

This book will be made available in paperback and on Kindle and the original three volumes will be withdrawn.

Thank you for taking the time to read this.

John Hilton, January 2019.

The Poems

7

Man in the Corner

He sits in the chair,
impassive gaze
falling upon nothing.
Unmoving.
Uncaring.
His lack of responsiveness
an unspoken threat.
His powerful hands,
resting in his lap,
in their stillness seem
the very currency of violence.
And yet,
behind those steel-blue eyes,
beyond the reach of his deep voice,
and underneath all the silence,
a little boy
from twenty long years ago
pleads
"Please help me,
I hurt."

1st March 2008

Picture in a Locket

You sit at the table with your coffee
staring for hours at a window
you do not see.
The sun has long since fallen

below the ranks of terrace houses
that mark the horizon of a life
that no longer seems your own.

The stars map the sky with diamonds but
there's no little jewel to point them out to
so you don't bother even seeing them.

You really should go to bed but
it seems doubly empty now.
He has left you and
she has gone for good.

You finger the locket that hangs
heavy around your bare neck
but you do not open it.

If only you could have found a way of
forgiving him for the unforgivable then
perhaps you would have been able to convince
yourself he was worth keeping?

But in the six months since, you
hadn't been able to think of a single
reason to ever trust him again.

But even his company would help now.
Any port in a storm,
now you're lost at sea,
abandoned by the lifeboats,
surrounded by sharks and

slowly drowning in your tears.

Perhaps you were a bad mother?
The whole street seems to think so.

Your baby cried.
You thought she was tired,
or maybe she was hungry?

She cried and cried,
but isn't that what babies
are supposed to do?

And then the crying stopped
you felt relieved.

Maybe things were better?

But they were not.

For your little angel
would never cry again.

You just didn't know.
Nobody wants to believe you
but you really didn't know.

Now you can't walk down
the street you live in,
trapped inside the place
you still call home

by the deafening whispers
and the killing stares.

Now you have no shoulder
to take your tears,
you have no angel
to take your love.

So you sit at the kitchen table
staring at a window onto a world
that you no longer want to see.

A world that has rejected you.

Next to your chest
lies a locket with
a photo of an angel.

You will never
open it again.

Your coffee has gone cold.
Somehow, it seems fitting.

14th August, 2009

And They Never Leave

You sit there and do your best.
A smile with more heartbreak
than any mount of tears.
Your voice tells me that things are fine

but your eyes they plead
"Please make them go away."

The room is silent.
The sounds of the ward
seem distant and unreal.
There are no voices to be heard
and yet your eyes still say
"Please make them go away"

Your mind crumples under those words
of which you are afraid to speak
as you sit deafened into dumbness
despite the silence that surrounds you.

You're cut off from the world,
safe from all those you fear.

But though the people come and go,
those voices
they never leave.

19ᵗʰ January, 2008

Bench by the Sea

I sat on the bench, near the seafront
the one we always sat in whenever
we returned from the beach together.
On warm afternoons we would sit
side by side, my arm around your
firm shoulders as we talked and

shared and had no need to look
into each others eyes as we did so.

But today this bench bears only one.
It is still the same bench and yet...

Sighing, I rise and walk back towards
the town and the journey home.

I doubt I will ever
sit there again.

14ᵗʰ January 2010

The Man in Number 27

An ordinary house
in an ordinary street.
Converted to flats
and rented to those
for whom the council
is willing to pay the rent.

And old Mrs Brown,
recently widowed, who lives
lonely in number seventeen
is now trapped completely
in her empty home,
unable to go along the street
to have her little chats
with the shop-keepers,
terrified that she will meet

him from number twenty seven.

She is cold,
she is frightened,
and she is alone.

The curtains twitch nervously
up and down the rainy street.
Hushed voices mumble through the air.
The new resident of number twenty seven
has got them talking,
has got them frightened.
He looks like a normal bloke,
same number of limbs,
same shape as people.
But the secret is out.

He is mad.

Loyal Daily Mail readers
up and down the street
know only too well
just what it means
when the mad move in.

They've read the headlines.
They've read the editorials.
And now they are waiting
for him to make his move.

And they are frightened;

for their children,
for their property,
and for their own sanity.

And nobody will tell them
just what is wrong with him,
only that he is mad.

And a word fills the street,
though nobody has spoken it.
That strange, barely understood
Greek-Latin mess of syllables
that plugs straight into
their very deepest fears.

Psychopath.

There.

It has been said.

And the curtains continue to twitch
as the frightened people
hide from a world they
simply cannot understand.

And in number twenty seven
is the new tenant.

George won prizes at school
for discipline and sport

and was known to all
as such a pleasant lad.

But those people are
so far from him now.
He's not even allowed
to contact his family
who no longer see him
as one of their own.

He sits in his second-hand armchair
staring unseeing at the borrowed TV.
He hasn't eaten in two days,
too scared to go to the shop
and face a world that he
can no longer relate to.
He just sits and doesn't see
the microscopic corner of the universe
in which he now exists.

Blood runs down the walls,
the doors scream at him
and the TV sucks his life
and his very soul out of him.

He is hungry,
he is scared
and he is alone.

Meanwhile,
in the sitting-room of number 12a,

seven ugly men sneer into their beer.
A correction is being planned.

5ᵗʰ September 2008

For Mrs Rigby's Children

You sit at home near the phone
but it doesn't ring
and it won't
unless there's a man in Bangalore
who wants to sell you a mobile phone
that will never ring either.

I write these words in anger.
Anger that there are too many people
to whom those words are not clichéd,
nor are they sentimental.
They are their life.

Perhaps they live in your street,
or lie forgotten in some dusty corner
of your phone book.

Perhaps they are your mother,
or maybe they're just some widower
alone now
and forgotten by all
but the tax man.

You have joy
and you have time.

Would it be too much to ask
for you to share a little bit?

26th December, 2007

Peace in My Time

Some days I get scared.

Sometimes it all seems black.

Other days it's just grey.

My mind can be a party,
other days a riot,
else it's gone away.

Fighting for the middle ground
didn't help me much,
dreading the blue
and frightened of the red.

Now I just let be.
Whoever I am today,
That's who I am.
I've still got scars but
at least the war has stopped.
For now.

10th September, 2007

Nostalgic Spiral

This morning I was thinking again
about how I miss the things that used
to be in those years when I was with you.

*Old decayed paths leading
to empty, dusty rooms full
of unchanging shadows.*

I was thinking about how I miss
the things that used to be in
those years when I was with you.

*I live in the present as
the past is gone and
the future has no form.*

I was thinking about how I miss
those years when I was with you.

*I try to move forward but I keep
looking over my shoulder and
tripping on every little gap.*

I was thinking about
how I miss you.

*Round and round as
the focus gets fainter
as the trench gets
deeper.*

I was thinking about you.

Reduction.
It seems less is
just less after all.

Thinking about you.

29th February 2012

Prison Cell For One *(Key Included)*

This is home.
Your home.

It's a nice place.
You've been happy here.

But not today.
Not for some time.

It's still the same.
Filled with all the
objects you loved.

But you hate it now.

You hate it because you
can no longer leave it.

The world goes by your window

but you cannot see any of it,
for the curtains stay closed
(it is simpler that way).

You get claustrophobic but
the outside world is much
too crowded for you now.

Too many people.
Too many eyes.

Too many shadows
and too many lights.

In here you are lonely,
but at least nobody
can see you cry.
In here you are helpless,
but at least nobody
can hear you scream.

The bills get paid by direct debit and
the food gets delivered to your door
in vans labelled Sainsbury's or Asda.
And the door remains safely locked
from the inside.

This is home.
Your home.

20th January 2010

The Lady in the Locked Room

I don't really understand what happened.

I admit that now just so you know.

I'm safe now, or so they tell me,
but I'm not quite sure who it is
I'm being kept safe from.
It all happened, and now they
insist that it wasn't like that.
I would start at the beginning but
there are too many of them and I
just can't get them into order.

I don't see how I could have known
when he invited me to meet
him over dinner at that little café
he liked to frequent that he
hadn't changed is mind and
was intending to ask me back.

We were so happy together.
Or at least I was happy.
He seemed distracted and
maybe he felt differently.
It wasn't my fault that
I just couldn't have kids.
Or maybe it was his fault?
I can't remember now.

After he told me that he wanted

to go away to another city I could
not understand what he was saying
and so I kept asking him where
we were going and he kept saying
I didn't understand and we
both got angry and I told him
I was not going to grant him
any kind of divorce and he got
very angry and then he shot me dead.

After months apart we both realised
that we still loved each other and
that we had to get back together
and stay together this time.

It was so wonderful and the
best time of my life even though
this seems to have happened after
he killed me which is strange.

It's the little details like this that are
giving me such difficulty when I try
to understand the things they tell me.

You have no idea how alone and
utterly without hope I felt that
day as I sat in that cold hotel
room all alone on the tenth floor with
just my memories and my hurt for
company and solace.
Everything that I lived for had been

taken away from me and now there
was nothing, I was just a shell with
no purpose and now meaning
so I smashed the tinted window
and jumped to my death.

All his friends and colleagues were
screaming at me and at each other
and there were gun shots and
more screams and then it was
quiet and I relaxed and sat
down on one of the stools
and waited for something
to happen, but for a while
nothing did.
Then some other men in uniform
came and they brought me here
and then they locked the door.

We were so beautiful together.
I knew almost as soon as we
began to talk that he was the
one for me and I think that
he thought the same and when
we first made love I swore that
he would always be mine
and I guess that I got my way.
There were other women but
they were easily disposed of.
He seemed to know his place
and so our love lasted forever.

That strange man and woman
in their suits came to talk to
me again today.
They keep trying to explain to
me why I am here even though
I tell them that I am happy and
don't want to be anywhere else.
Whenever I ask them when they
are going to arrest him for killing
me they just look frustrated and
keep insisting that I know why
they can't do that and then they
tell me that he's dead but when
I ask them how he died they
just say that I know full well
which is silly, because I wouldn't
ask the question if I knew.
And then they leave and
they lock the door once more.

I still don't understand what happened,
but at least I'm safe from him now.

31ˢᵗ January 2009

My Blood Like a Fire-Storm

Suddenly
the months of grey
empty long night

are blown away,
for today,
right here, right now
I know I can
do anything I want.

My only hindrance,
other people's doubts.

But they'll just have to
adjust to the now that
pumps through my body,
surging and urging
me to grab at any
dream that comes my way.

No-one will I allow
to question or challenge
what I know is here.

The world around me
glows and beckons
me ever outward,
it is not my fault
if their dreams
do not burn as bright
as the blood
that rages through my body,
like a fire-storm
that burns all I touch.

Circa 1994

A Child's Fear of the Dark

It is quiet,
as I lay here
alone.
All of the lights are off
and the sun now shines on Australia,
and a silence surrounds me,
envelops me,
imprisons me.
And my mind senses
all the terror
that lies
in the dark
silent
unknown reaches
of my imagination.
Am I really so silly
if I think the creatures
in my mind
really could
really kill me?

Circa 2000

Susan Makes Her Mark

Yesterday I stacked shelves.
Today I am doing the same.
And tomorrow?

Ah, sweet tomorrow....

Who am I?
I'm barely worth a number
much less a name.
But tomorrow...
Oh, for tomorrow...

I'm one of ten kids
My desperate mother
could barely remember
who we were
let alone
whose dad was whose.

I was number eight
But not tomorrow
and never again.

I had a lover once.
Said I was his Number One
It ended when I realised I was
just a number once more...

But tomorrow I shall be free.
Oh, yes.
No more this slow, living death.
Oh too feel the wind
blowing my cares away

-

Now here I stand
beyond the grasp
of all that held me down,
all that trapped me and
all that kept me small.

I look around at at this city below
that was never any kind of home.
At the rows of houses where
my life was doomed to never happen.
Pure joy surges through my body
as I run towards my
one chance of freedom.
Then over the final barrier
as I take this last chance
to leap towards Heaven...

21st June, 2007

Time Seeps Away

The world retreats
and a particular kind of silence descends
as I become more aware
of the crowded emptiness
that fills every corner
and every portrait
in which I choose to live.

All feels somehow
more distant

as if the interface
between the little world
of the flat I call home
and the big, wide world outside
has closed down
due to lack of interest.

I sit here in my bedroom,
the outside world
now like a memory
or a fantasy
that is no longer
of any particular concern to me.

Even my very body
has the feel of a prison
that holds me trapped
within its slow, aching grip.

My flat is silent,
my mind feels grey,
my coffee is cold,
As my time seeps away.

Unused.

Unheeded.

Wasted.

14th August 2008

Won't you sit and have a drink with me?

It's quiet today,
not many around
and I like to talk though
I don't really have much to say.

Won't you stay and have a drink with me?
I'm one or two ahead.
They help to calm my nerves
and quiet the voices in my head.

Won't you sit and have a drink with me
now that I'm all alone?
Help me forget the pangs
of a guilt I cannot atone?

Won't you stay and have a drink with me?
I need a few more than this,
to numb the pain
and stop the strain
of living my lie like this.

Won't you sit and have a drink with me?
A few jars for old times' sake?
Or just call me John the Baptist,
and serve me on a plate.

Circa 1996

Dreaming the Past Away

There must have been a time
Before the folds of my life became
echoed in my forehead creases.
When life was *here* and *now,*
not *then* or *there*
nor *him* nor *her*
or *was* but *isn't.*

It was *will be* and *is,*
missing instead of missed.
Before *lived* took the place of *living*
and *desires* were replaced by mere needs.

Passion was a *fire* before its embers became a tale.
Success was an ever-changing series of dreams
until it lost out to safety and the fear of failure.
And tired became weary,
cutting wit became bitter drone
and lonely drifted slowly into being alone.

There was a time when my dreams
were a source of great visions.
Now I merely wait for sleep
to pass the night away 'til the morning

12th June 2008

Levelling the Score

I see the face clearly as
it looks straight back at me.
Around the eyes swirl pain
and from the eyes spear rage.
Hard lips braced
poised to snarl.
As I look back
my eyes narrow,
brow lowers
and the menace
before implicit
comes forward.
The point of focus
piercing into my mind
What now?
What next?
The future
like the face before me
seems uncertain
and tinted with red.
Something,
somewhere
is going to give.
The gaze intensifies,
my face is steel and
my breathing
becomes studied
and deep.
And
at that moment

something gives.
I hear a growl
growing,
deepening.
The time is now.
I take a measured pace backwards.
Barked commands
guide my path.
The words have been spoken
and something has given.
I take another measured pace backwards.
Now I can see myself clearer
and I know the path I must take.
The future is coming
and it's tinted in red.
For blood has been raised
so blood must be spilt.
I put on my jacket
collect the tools
and get ready to leave my house
to restore the balance
in the blood.
The future is on its way
and tinted with red.
I shall bring it forth.

2007

How Mad Am I?

Hello?
Am I mad?

Well I guess that
in a certain light
I may appear to be so.

Well, in truth I'm so far
round the bend I've already
lapped myself seven times.

I've been unhinged so long
I've lost track of the door.

There are so few cups
left in my cupboard
I have to do my thinking
in plastic beakers now.

My loose screw fell out
so long ago it is
now being used
to support a bookshelf.

Been nuts so long
the squirrels think I'm a larder.

I'm so far off my trolley
it's been lent out to a tea lady.

I've been in cloud-cuckoo-land
so long I've started feeling
broody for my neighbours' nests.

Am so many bricks short of a wall
I'm starting to count foundations.

Been barking at the moon so much it
has started throwing sticks for me to chase.

I've been in the barmy-army so long
I've been promoted to wing-commander.

But, other than that,
I'm as sane as you.

Say 'hello'.

9th November 2008

Debris

This is where it ends.

A bitter old man
in a tiny, dirty flat
raging to nobody
about a world
that has left him behind.

He survived the wars.
He lived through the sixties.

He endured the seventies.
He hid in the eighties.
He shivered through the nineties.
But he knows he
won't survive this.

He realises that when
he has breathed his last,
at most he will be remembered
by a few strangers
as the daft old bugger
from the flat on the fourth floor
who drank too much cheap vodka,
smoked too many dog-ends
and shouted at a world
that was not interested in hearing
his spiteful
hateful
empty
painful
screams.

Time's wave moves ever on.
Welcome to the debris
abandoned in its wake.

27th April, 2007

In the Breeze

My legs kick hard
in a failing attempt
to keep my head
above the water.

I am drowning.

My dam of self-control
has been breeched
at ground level
and the dark seas
of my dreams
and of my fears and tears
floods into the room.

I am drowning in the attic.

My life is aflame,
consuming itself
as the line between
self -expression
and self-destruction
blurs and then dissolves
and once again
I find myself
drowning in the attic
of the house of fire.

18th August 2008

Smoke Room in the Mad Ward

The smoke curled round us
as we sat in the smoke room
beneath a sepia ceiling

that has looked down
on so much despair.

She sat opposite me
drawing on her Berkley menthol.
Each puff
bringing her closer
to the only relief
she had left to
look forward to.
She looked at me
her eyes windows
on a soul that was trying
to cry itself out of existence,
a look that had become familiar to me
from the bathroom mirror.

"If only I could close my eyes
and dream.
Dream of walking through a meadow
or just sitting on an old tree
at the edge of a wood",
she sighed.
Her pain flowed over
and whispered down her cheeks.

I held out my hand
and into it she trusted hers.
Her eyes queried this small union
then her gaze lifted to mine
and slowly her face
hesitatingly brightened into a smile.
A smile that spoke
of two strangers
sharing two hurts
too deep to ever be spoken.

The moment flowed through several minutes

Presently her voice caressed
"Thank you
for letting me share
without asking
what it was"

I smiled my thanks
raised her hand to her cheek
kissed her forehead
and we parted.

I returned to my bed
warmed by the knowledge
that for those few minutes
we had been closer than lovers
and warmer than the sun

For now I could hear the wood

and she could see the meadow....

13th July, 2007

Listening

I have no answers for you,
only you have your own.
Sometimes the only way
you will are able to hear them
is when you can find somebody
to tell them to.

8th December, 2007

Go For It!

The overwhelming courage
underpinned
by a not so hidden aggression
and coloured by a sheen
of capricious ebullience.

Circa 1995

Just Another Bad Day

I hear voices in the hall
laying plans for my doom.
How they'll hide my body
and be gone before the dawn
But don't let this disturb you
is all the nurses say.

There's nothing here to concern you.
It's just another bad day

The walls are growing arms now,
fingernails dripping blood
and the room is slowly shrinking
while my head prepares to explode.
But there's nothing to be frightened of
they only want to play.
Nothing here for anyone to see.
It's just another bad day.

The voices bark out their orders
that I've been told to ignore.
And night goes on forever regardless
of what the sun has to say.
But there's no need to pay heed to
voices that have too much to say.
Just swallow these little pills for
we know you've just had another
of your very own bad days.

5th November, 2007

These Walls Have Seen Tears

He waited half a lifetime for somebody
who could give him permission to scream
and maybe then allow him to cry.
But that person never appeared and
one grey and wet Autumn morning
he realised he would have to invent

this person or go under.

O shadows that hide in the dark
come forth into the grey light so
I may see your shape and try to
understand the glow that seems
to give you shape and form.

I continue walking because it is
what I do and defines almost all
that I am or am likely to be.
Force of habit is mere detail.

And in my dream there is an ending,
a distinct destination and a reason for
all this seemingly endless walking
living ever on.

But not here,
not now and
not in any waking moment
ever.

Too many years have passed since
any dream of mine started with a
beginning as now there are just
endless continuations and repeats.

Memories?
Visions?
Ghosts?

Madness?

The words you choose are not important.

It is very easy to cut yourself on
the sharp edges of these dreams.
So flee into the apparent safety
of wakefulness if you want but
we know you must return and
you must know that we are
waiting, for we can wait for
a long time as we have great
patience.

I tried living my dream but found
there was no way of dreaming
another into it and then discovered
there is no rising from a waking
dream and when you have no hand
to hold a dreamed embrace is a poor
substitute.

Live now,
not then nor
in the never-never,
but right here,
right now.

For what was
is no more and
what may be

might be.
What is,
is what we have.

This wall has two sides,
would you not like to see
what is on the other?

30th October 2010

Left Them Tracks

I'm running through this night
at a hundred miles an hour
I'm going to stop for nobody,
you know I'm at my best this way.

Threw out my brakes a while back
and got plenty more coal to burn.
Furnace is flaming white hot
and my shovel's just a blur.

This engine keep on running
till there's nothing left to burn.
My body is on fire
and love drives this engine on.
I just ain't gonna tire
until it all my love is gone.

I got no need for mainlines
while my body sings this song.
I'm running through this night

past one hundred miles an hour
as mind drives onward and on.

But my tender's running low babe,
I'll be all spent one day.
But I'm not brave enough to stop,
so it has to be this way.

7th September 2008

Sonata for Empty Pillow

For twenty four years or a couple short of
eternity I have lay here alone just waiting
for a return that will never happen.

The dust stars dance a slow waltz in the early
morning rays as my breath sighs a slow rhythm.

A muted dawn chorus sings a requiem duet with
the distant traffic hum as I sink further into the
unbalanced contours of this half empty bed.

You were always so free and so alive that I
always assumed that you'd live forever as if
no other possibility could even be considered.

I can hear your voice now, as soft as silk, as warm
as summer sun and as strong as the roots that
break the concrete of those pavements that you
so recently glided along, gracing all that saw
you with the essence of life that you gave

to all those around you so freely.

But half of this bed is cold,
and the rest merely occupied
and little warmer.

Sometimes when I lie awake, the room
fades around me and I can see only her face.
All else seems ghostlike and of no particular
relevance as I roll over onto my left to face
that pink pillow that you always favoured and
where memory of your long golden-blond hair
with your brown eyes sparkling in your deep
brown complexion with those lips so full of love
and life sings so softly yet firmly of your absence.

So I roll back over and out of our bed,
needlessly reminding myself as I do,
there will only be one
for breakfast again today.

7th March 2009

Fright or Flight

I could run from here,
flee into the big wide world
which I'm assured exists
beyond the curtained portals
of my windows.

I could visit those places

I see on the maps
that line my walls.
Meet some of those people
who populate this world
of which I have heard so much
yet understood so little.

There's oceans and there's mountains,
rivers and ravines,
cities of great buildings,
forests of old trees.

Roads and other pathways
to take me to wherever
they want me to go.

But here I sit
still in this chair,
unmoved from this room.

The world is outside
and I am within.

For here I cannot drown in those seas
or fall from those mountain tops.

Those people cannot see me
as I weep words onto paper.

The trees will grow and fall
whether I glimpse them or not

and the roads have plenty
of passengers already.

I know exactly where
I am not going
and I see what my life
has inevitably become.

But I also know that
there is no number
safer than one

25th October 2008

The Necessity of Speed

Why bother with tomorrow
when there's so much I can do now?
Bouncing from one job to another,
raising my game,
running on the spot,
trying to out run the fast lane.
Forget about recuperation
just keep the coffee and
the chocolate stocked up.
And why should I care about
the ends of that candle you mention?
Time passes swiftly
and if I slow down I'll miss the bus.
You worship your God
I'll stick with caffeine and adrenaline.
But deep down I know you are right

that sooner or later
one way or another
I am going to have to stop.
But why worry about tomorrow
when there's so much to do today?

15th January, 2008

The Feel of Goodbye

So this is what goodbye feels like?

It feels hollow
like a space
inside me
that will resist filling.

Like a hole
that my tongue keeps probing
even though it hurts.

So must we?

Can we not say 'hello' instead?

Circa 1993

Levelling the Score 2

You see the face clearly
as it looks straight at you.
Around your eyes swirl pain

and from your eyes spears rage.
Hard lips braced,
poised to snarl.
Now look back.
Narrow your eyes.
Lower your brow.
Bring the menace,
before implicit,
forward.
Pierce the point of focus
into your mind.

What now?
What next?
The future
like the face before you
seems uncertain
and tinted with red.

Something,
somewhere,
is going to give.
Feel the gazes intensify
as faces steel.
Make your breathing
studied and deep.
At that moment
something will give.

Hear a growl
growing

deepening.
The time is now.
Take a measured pace backwards.
Let barked commands
guide your path.
The words have been spoken
and something has given.

Take another measured pace backwards.
Now see yourself clearer
and know the path that you must take.
The future is coming
and it's tinted in red.
For blood has been raised,
so blood must be spilt.

Put on your jacket,
collect the tools
and get ready to leave your house.
Restore the balance
in the blood.

The future is on its way
and tinted with red.

You must bring it forth.

2007

Words to a Friend.

You tell me
that you are old.
That life has left you behind.
That you feel
like damaged goods.
And with clumsy words
I try to tell you that
although it hurts you
when you cry
and scares you
when you rage,
although it's cold
outside your womb,
and though it bites
to see your age,
I know your life
has left its scars but
all these things
make you what you are
and are the reasons
your friends love you.

And a painting in progress
is far more interesting
and more beautiful
than an empty canvas.

Circa 1996

When I Close My Eyes too Long

When I close my eyes too long
the world darkens,
turns red
and they come out to play
their games of hate
and blood
and death.

When I close my eyes too long
I see the faces
of those I love
who are now departed
shredded and bloodied
and racked with pain.

And when I open them again
they have gone,
the sun shines
and I see no blood.

But no matter how I shake my head
still each and everyone are dead.

30th April, 2007

A Child's Last Prayer

Dear God,
I'm sorry I've been a bad girl
I don't mean to be,

but sometimes I forget.

Please don't hurt me any more.

Is Mr Buchan really an angel?
He says that he is.
He says that he is helping me
to be a good girl
by punishing me when I'm bad.

But he hurts me
and makes me cry,
and if I tell my daddy
he'll make my daddy die.

So will you please tell daddy
so he can make it stop?

I really will try
to be good
but I don't know
if I can do it.

Please, please Mr God,
don't hurt me any more.
I hurt so much already.

Father David says that
you love everybody.
But that means that
you love Mr Buchan.

And I hurt so much already.

Please God,
just one last wish.

I know it's not my time yet,
but will you forgive me
if I join you now?

20th September, 2006.

Bitter

Oh, what have we done?
Kindness it would seem
is out of fashion.
Any attempt at sympathy
either dismissed as uncool
or attacked as 'PC'.
I see those around me
using each other
as no more than fuel
for their inflated egos.
Searching out easy targets,
living out Thatcher's Me Me Me.
These days Love Thy Neighbour
means shagging the woman next door
and Armageddon no more
than an excuse to do nothing
in the vain hope that God
will sort it all out on our behalf.

Sometimes I wonder if
there will be anything worthwhile left
for the meek to inherit...

27ᵗʰ April, 2007

The Woman in the Chair

She sits in the chair
seeming just another relic
turning slowly to dust.

Her hands rest on her knees,
eyes face towards the window,
but her focus is a world away
from the trimmed lawns
and prim flower beds.

But behind those dry eyes
is another world.

A world that has passed
and yet lives on within.

Its sights, sounds and smells
and all those people
live and breathe and love
in a mind now cut adrift
from a world that has become
shadowy and unreal to her.

A warm smile fills her mind

but cannot be seen
from the outside.

Every two hours they add tablets
to another old woman
in another well worn chair.

She takes up that little bit of space
but her eyes hide her little secret.

She isn't really there.

2nd February, 2008

Like a Sun Rising

The lonely and
the dispossessed,
the heartbroken,
the frightened
and the worried.
All are welcome here.
For I have been all of those things
and know all too well
how it can feel.
I don't have any answers
and I can't supply solutions,
but I know how to listen
and I know how to hear.
And seeing a face
that was wet with tears
break into a smile

like a sun rising over ashes
makes my world a little warmer
and my life a little fuller.

2nd April, 2007.

Anaesthesia

These days I sit
and watch my life
from the outside
and feel so very cold.
I must confess such things
matter to me no more.

I am alone and yet I know
it is always better this way.

Please let me truly feel
the things I felt before
my heart concealed
all the hurt and all
the war within my soul,
a soul so bruised and torn.
There's no refunds or returns
once you have been born.

I now want to feel all

my pain and so much more,
so I can heal all those things
that I broke before,
when I was filled with fear
and held nothing dear.

Now I fear the pain much less
than I dread feeling numb.
Won't you please allow
me to feel anything at all?
Show me there is some hope
that there will be an end
to this damned war.

So I sit here and
watch my life
from the outside as
there's no place left
to live within.

8ᵗʰ August 2017

A Midnight Quiet

It is nearly midnight and
the silence is so close to
complete as to allow the
sound of my heartbeat

to be heard at last.

I am so very tired and
every second seems to last
for a lifetime as the thuds
from my heart appear to move
further apart even as they grow
less urgent and deeper in tone.

Through my window I can see
only vague shadows below and
a scattering of stars above.

Inside this little room I sit in
a darkness free from stars and
shadows and interrupted only by
the red glow of my alarm clock.

The illuminated display silently
changes from 11:59 to 12:00.

It is midnight and
nothing has happened and
nothing has changed.

But I no longer have any real
interest in events or changes

of any sort as it is only endings
hold interest for me now.

I breathe in.

I breathe out.

My lifetime passes every second.

My heart has long
since stopped roaring
and now only murmurs
what passes for
it's passions.

Midnight has now passed and
and new day will presently
emerge over the horizon.

It doesn't matter and
I no longer care.

All around me
remains in darkness
and in silence.

15th September, 2016.

Razor Blades and Other Pain Killers

Openings

Hello my dear friend.
Well, I know am making
a rather large assumption,
but I hope anybody who
chooses to read this does
so as some kind of friend.
Maybe there is still,
after all that has
happened,
a little part of me
that is sufficiently naive?
I truly hope so.
I really do.

Regardless,
my name is Χγн.
Yeah, I know.
Just don't worry
about it as almost
nobody else knows
how to pronounce
it, but at least you
care enough to ask.

I digress, please
do accept my
humble apology.

My name, as I
have already said,
is Xүн and I am
one of those people
you read about who
waste so much of
our doctor's time by
deliberately causing
myself injuries.

If I must be judged
then I'd much rather
do it myself, thank you.

This is my room,
my place of safety.
This is where I
deal with the worst
of my problems,
the darkest of
my pain.
This is no childish gesture

or attention-seeking whim.

This is how I have learnt
to cope with things I am
not even allowed to admit
ever happened.

Do you have any idea
what that feels like?
To have a pain so great
it rips your mind into
jagged shreds and yet
to have to pretend nothing
really happened?

No,
of course you do not.
Why should you?

Suffering is a sequence
of events, not an
achievement.

So, here I sit in my
little, wooden chair,
in front of the unit
that serves both as

my dressing table
and as a table for
my dressings.

This evening it has,
as so many previous
occasions over the years,
been carefully prepared
for a relief session.

But I would not want
you to think these things
to be trivial and the
complex ritual to be
the sort of thing I do
on a weekly basis.

Only when the pain
and the voices and
the desire to bring
an end to all this
becomes almost,
but not quite,
overwhelming,
do I remove my
equipment from
its hiding place in

the back of the
airing cupboard
and go through the
precisely orchestrated
steps I know will bring
me the only relief I
have ever known.

All of the usual objects
have been removed from
the top of the dresser and
a white cloth of purity and
sterility placed over it.
The cloth is quite thick
and though it has been
through a dozen wash
cycles it is still as white
and reassuringly clean
as it was when I
smuggled it into
what was then
my parent's home
all those years ago.

Upon this not so
virginal cloth rests
three blades, each

sharpened to the
level of sharpness
normally associated
with scalpels.
These sit in a metal
kidney bowl of the
type you see in
surgical theatres.
The bowl is, as I
should not need to
stress, meticulously
cleaned and polished.
To the right of this sits
a larger bowl filled with
warm water tinted with a
precisely measure dose
of antiseptic.
Along the back lie
the dressings and
bandages I will
require for the last
stages of my
treatment.
Finally,
tucked into the far corner
is the needle and thread
I have, thankfully, yet

to require.
I am too careful for that
to occur very often
but not so cock-sure
as to leave them off
the dresser.
Sometimes safer
really is better
than sorry.

I'll not bore you with
unnecessary descriptions
of the procedure,
suffice to say
there are usually
three, in extreme
cases four or at the
most five, lines of
relief that will require
all the nurturing and
loving care I have
never received from
any body else.

No,
I don't want pity
or even sympathy

from you or from
anybody else.

I deal with this myself.
That is the whole point
of what I do.

I went through those things
by myself and I
will get through this
the same way.

That is all for now
as I have a process
to complete and it
requires all of my
concentration.

It is also private.

Goodbye.

Beginnings
By the age of ten I had
learnt how to deal with
the voices, the pain, the
shame and the unfortunate

mess associated with the
ritual, until one evening,
after an hour or so of peace
and something approaching
tranquillity, I was called
down by my mother to take
part in one of those strange
and possibly fashionable
late suppers she sprung upon
the household at seemingly
random intervals, I forgot
in my haste to comply to
properly cover up all the
marks and spillages and
predictably, when my mother
saw the cuts she immediately
and forcibly demanded to
know what exactly I had done
and precisely why I had done it.

For some reason I will
probably never really
understand it simply
did not occur to me
to lie about these things
or try to cover them up
with long sleeves,

thin excuses and
facile and fragile
justifications.

She was not impressed.

She even claimed to be
deeply shocked by what
she saw that evening.

I'd come home with
far worse injuries
following a fall or
fight in the playground
and she had not batted
an eyelid so why all
the fuss now?

I could not understand
what the problem was.
Just a few lines made
with a pin.
They weren't deep and
didn't even require a
plaster let alone any
stitches and yet my
mother recoiled in

horror as if I had
mutilated myself
beyond recognition.

As was often her way,
she shifted gears from
shocked to horrified to
extremely angry in
quick succession.

In truth, after a minute
or so I just switched my
self off to the world
around me and let her
screams and her blows
fall unheard and unfelt.

I didn't understand why
my coping strategies
shocked and angered her
so then and I don't really
understand why so many
are upset by them still.

It's not as if I go around
hurting people is it?

And no, it is not true
to suggest that I hurt
myself as the whole
point of what I do is
to reduce pain.

Sometimes I wonder
why I bother trying
to explain these things
as it has been made
clear to me on so very
many occasions that
the world I live in that
I am apparently expected
to think of as home
does not want to hear,
let alone think about,
how a person like me
learns to live with and
as a person like me.

Don't bother as I
didn't expect to be
understood.

The thing that angers me
the most is the punishment.

Why?
What is so awful about
learning to cope with
things most people don't
even have to think about
in ways that are carried
out behind close doors
so as not to cause offence
and don't really hurt
anybody anyway?

I don't know and I
am not sure if I
care any more.

Continuance
Come on, man,
just give me a
break.

It is not a big deal.

Things have been
getting a bit heavy
recently so I just
carried out a few

procedures to help
me deal with things
and get through the
day without falling
apart at the seems.

Let us try to keep this
thing in perspective,
it is not like I've been
snorting crack cocaine
or jacking up heroin,
is it?

I *could* be getting drunk
and getting into fights
and beating my kids
when I finally get
home from the pub.

But no, instead I choose
to make a few marks
that don't hurt anybody
and aren't dangerous
and shouldn't be any
skin off your nose
anyway.

If you don't want
to see then I suggest
you stop looking.

All I hear is nonsense
about how I could be
spreading various
diseases they don't
even have the courage
to put a name to.

It's not about retaining
childish responses to
difficult situations it
is about knowing what
works for me and how
to make the most of
the resources I have
to cope with all the
pressures involved in
living my life in this
body and with this
mind of mine.

I have spent hundreds,
and I do mean hundreds,
of hours in libraries and

lately on the internet
researching methods
for achieving the most
effective release patterns
with the lowest treatment
requiring injury profiles.

That probably sounds a bit
odd if not dark and rather
disturbing to you but
that is your problem
and I have enough
of my own,
thank you.

Adverse Remedies

I don't have a problem so
why should I accept help?
Doing things in a different
manner is not the same as
doing things the wrong way.
I understand the methods I
choose to use to distract from
the pain and improve the focus
of my mind probably seem
quite shocking to you, but
nobody has so far been able

to suggest any alternative
techniques that would
actually help me to deal
with my particular set of
problems as effectively
and efficiently as the blade.
What I cannot understand
is why those doctors who
run this establishment and
into whose care I have been
placed do not seem able to
comprehend the simple and
frankly obvious reasons why
their preventing me from
carrying out any of my coping
strategies has resulted in a
deterioration of my condition
as my ability and desire to
communicate with and function
within a small social group,
namely the in-patients currently
on this ward has degenerated
to a clear and substantial degree.
Apparently it is causing the
aforementioned doctors a
considerable amount of
worry and concern.

I've told them time
and time again what
is needed but, even
though I have explained
to them in simple terms
even they should be able
to understand, how a
few, discrete and non
threatening procedures,
using the sterilised tools
they could, without particular
difficulty or even significant
cost, make available to me,
would bring about a release
of the mental pressure and
allow them to tick several
of those boxes that allow
them to claim some kind
of success in the so-called
fight against mental health
problems and difficulties.
See?
I am not just thinking of
myself but also trying to
make those professionals
into whose care I was
forced by those well

meaning policemen, look
like they actually have
some vague idea
what they are doing.

Of course I am aware
they are highly trained,
but then so are those
dogs that perform tricks
in circuses, and yet you
wouldn't expect me to
make life changing
decisions based largely
on the advice of highly
trained dogs,
would you?

Of course,
the doctors have learnt
far more complicated
tricks than the dogs but
the process is more or
less the same if you
focus on the teaching
methods employed
and the results.
In each case you end

up with a number of
performing animals
arranged in packs
around an alpha male
or senior consultant
as the medical profession
calls their equivalent.
Why is it wrong for me
to use a knife in the
course of my therapy
and yet perfectly acceptable
for a surgeon to use a scalpel
to cut deep into the body and
remove bits from within?

How is it different?
Both are done to cure a
person of ills.
Whether you are comfortable
with it or not, it is a simple
fact that it *does* help me to
cope with things and your
disapproval does nothing to
reduce its effectiveness.

Wrong.
You are right that I am

suffering and suffering
greatly, but the reason
for that suffering is that
you have taken away the
only treatment available
to me that actually works
and also the only crutch
I know will support me.
So, no,
I don't particularly want
to thank you for what
you have done for me.

If you want to help me
I'd suggest the best thing
you could do is to sign
me off your books, let
me go and stay the hell
out of my life.

Yes,
I am taking this seriously.
I know how to deal with
this but you and your
colleagues are preventing
me from undergoing the
treatment I need.

So damn you all and
leave me alone.

Yer Blues

The year did not get
off to a good start as
my life changed from
a painfully dull realist
novel to a particularly
bad blues song.
You know the ones
I'm talking about.
My love ran away
with my best friend,
I lost my job when
my firm went bust
and my cat died.
I'd laugh if only I could
work out how to cry.
I've never been good
at emotional responses
to events and I guess
that is why I am on
my own once more.
You could describe,
if documenting such

things appeals to you,
the six month car crash
that followed these events
as a major relapse or some
similar cliched nonsense.
There was certainly plenty
of blood and glass involved.
Nothing like turning a tragedy
into a splatter movie, is there?
I cannot honest say I blame
my other half for walking
away from our not so
sweet home any more
than I blame my best
friend for taking them in.
As I think I mentioned
earlier on, I have never
been comfortable with
the idea of displaying or
acting upon emotional
responses and I guess
that might make me
appear somewhat cold
and slightly distant.
But who am I trying
to kid here?
The reason I appear that way

is because I *am* cold and distant.
But it wasn't all about
glass and blood,
far from it,
there were some sharp bits
of metal involved as well.
Oh?
So even grim and realist humour
has to be *appropriate* now?
I was just trying to make
the point that there was much
more to that year than using
broken bottles for a bit of
improvised surgery.
Really?
Then I suppose you could
try thinking of it as a kind
of negative cosmetic surgery.
Come on, now.
You honestly think most
plastic and/or cosmetic
surgery is carried out
for medical reasons?
I don't know what world
you are living in but it
is not one I'm familiar with.
Professionals?

Safe?
You are just too
weird for words.
If you find my answers so
difficult and distasteful
then I suggest you think
more carefully about the
type of questions you
want to ask me.

Survival

Why on Earth would I
want to be young again?
Why would I want to
replace one set of mistakes
with another set?
No,
I don't think there is any
real point in dreaming
about how things might
be if this or that had not
happened.
What happened cannot
be changed and what
didn't occur has missed
its chance.
Things are as they are.

Hoping they would
somehow magically
become different, and
you presume better, is
mere delusion.
Yes,
obviously I remember
being younger.
No, not everything.
Very little, in fact.
But I do remember
significant parts of it
all too clearly and
those memories are
enough to make me
glad I don't remember
any more.
Memories are both what
we were and what we
have since become.
Alright, let me put it
this way.
What we are now is
a product of all we
have seen and heard
and done and had
done to us.

And you must realise
it is not necessary to
remember the events
for them to have such
profound effects on how
you progress through life.
Sometimes we can choose
the things that happen to
us but other times we can
only choose how we respond
to events that are otherwise
beyond our control.
There is no such thing as luck,
there are only those who take
responsibility for their lives,
those who simply look outward
for the source of their so called
bad luck and lastly, the majority,
who fall between those two
ends of the blame spectrum.
Since I don't really understand
why those things happened I
cannot even begin to decide
how to distribute the blame
and the responsibility.
Such is life.
Sometimes shit just happens.

There is no reason for it.
It serves no purpose.
It has nothing to do with
curses or omens or whatever
and it can't be measured in
balances of karma either.
Whether or not you choose
to accept things as they are
or if you prefer to search
for blame and responsibility
for every little thing that
happens makes no difference
to events as they will happen
regardless of any acceptance
on your part.

The Healing Wound

Yes, I do understand how
causing injuries in order
to make a person better
might appear to run
counter to what is
generally accepted
as common sense.
And yet that is what
surgeons do everyday
without anybody becoming

upset or angry or questioning
their motives.
And what people like me
do when the need arises
is not really that different.
It may be seen as somewhat
less than conventional but it
gets the job done and means
we don't have to rely on
professionals to get us
through our days.
And do tell me what
punching pillows is
supposed to achieve?
We cope with things
because we deal with
our problems ourselves.
A few scratches are not
in themselves a problem.
It is, as it pretty much
always is, other people
who are the problem.
It is their attitudes and
judge-mentalism, not our
actions, that are the root
of the conflict.
We do not require nor seek

their approval so it is not
theirs to grant or withhold.
I *do* look after myself.
That is the whole point.
It is the application of
the blade that allows me
to cherish that part of me
with the tender loving care
I missed out on when I was
so much younger.
The mere hurt of a few
incisions is nothing when
compared to the screams
and blood of the darkest
of memories.
There are no bandages for
torn memories or bleeding
dreams of trauma.
Of course I know
what I am doing.
I've been perfecting this
technique since I was
eleven years old.
It took me a while
to get things just
right as there was
no internet to look

up the right tools
and techniques for
the job but I think
I am getting rather
good at it now.

Filled to Bursting

No,
to be honest I have
no idea what you
hoped to achieve
by bringing me to
this place of alleged
safety.
Who are you to think
you have the right to
protect us from ourselves?
It doesn't help in the long
run and even in the short
term it is doomed to fail.
The staff's attempts to
keep me safe from my
so-called destructive
urges were at best
ineffective and at times
frankly laughable.
They took down a glass

framed picture but gave
no thought to the window
panes in my room.
They stopped me using a
knife at mealtimes not
thinking about the damage
I could do with a fork.
All right.
OK.
Enough
already.
I know what I do is
no more than a
temporary measure
that has gone on for
perhaps longer than
is wise but what else
can anybody offer me
that will relieve any
of the pressure of
memory that builds
up inside me?
How else can I force
the focus of my mind
away from those dark
regions of memory and
onto the world that will

carry on turning wherever
my focus may lie?
I'm not terrible and
nor am I special, I
don't see why you
can't accept that I
am just an ordinary
human being.
How many times do I
have to tell you that I
don't want your pity and
your sympathy is lacking
in any degree of empathy
and serves merely to
demonstrate your inability
to understand any of this?
There is nothing worthwhile
to be gained from you endlessly
inventing alleged flaws in
my current methods of therapy
until you can come up with
a truly viable alternative.
Acceptance?
Of what?
Name me on occasion
upon which I have denied
any of those unpleasant

things that were done to
my childhood self.
Wrong.
To come to terms requires
two people, who can then
come to some kind of
agreement.
How do you expect me
to get those dark corners
of my mind to agree to
anything let alone arrange
a truce or ceasefire?
I am not at war with myself.
Such talk is at best nonsense.
A war suggests at least
two sets of people and
in this there is only me.
It's kind of lonely standing
on a battlefield waiting
for an enemy who has
never existed.
There are no bodies and
the desolation is no more
than the dead forms of
what were previously
real feelings.
The only feeling I can

relate to now come
from sharp edges.

Walk Away

Why should I agree to
any of your suggestions.
It's my life and I
would rather live
it my way.
I think I have reached
the point when I am
strong enough to make
my own choices and
take some kind of
control over my life.

That is the point.
To choose between a
selection of ideas you
brought to the table
is to pick one of *your*
choices.
If I'm going to make
my *own* choices then
I have to work out
for myself what those
choices are.

It's not just about choice
of treatment it is also
about deciding for myself
which road I want to walk
along or even if I want to
walk at all.
But I am frightened.
I've always tried to do
what I think people want
me to do, act in ways I
hope will make them
happier.
Now I am trying to work out
how to do things for me and
that means taking responsibility
for the choices I make.
Mostly I need to start to feel
things once more.
Everything I have done for
the last twenty whatever years
has been about blotting out
feelings and I guess the idea
of actually feeling things is
what frightens me most of all.
I appreciate you have clearly
spent a lot of time putting
together those three treatment

programs for me but I really
don't know how to choose.
I'll need to think for a while.

[note: after a few minutes silence,
the subject simply stood up
and left the room]

16ᵗʰ June, 2016

Song From the Edge of Forever

This is a song from the place
where hearts go when they break.
Where love goes to die and
and learns the price of hate.

This is my song from the edge of forever.
A desperate plea that we will never
lose sight of the beauty and love
as found both below and above.
This song I give you with love
from the very edge of forever.

This is a song from the time
young hearts grow old and grey.
When hope begins to fade
and joy just flies away.

This is my song of despair.
Will we ever really dare
to openly love all this is here
without ego, lust or fear?

Here dreams are all dark and hope
is nowhere to be seen and yet
somewhere there is a place where
we will find plenty to remember
and nothing we need to forget.
.
So sing this song from the edge of forever
Do our best to ensure that we never
lose sight of the beauty and love
as found both below and above.
Sing this song with love and joy
from the very heart of forever.

30th November 2017

Sound of Blue

She looked up at me and asked
"So, what sound does blue make?"

She always knows how to ask
the right questions and I can only
be proud of such a grand-daughter.
But how to answer this one?
I think back to the days when
her voice was more than just

lip movements and expression.
Ah, but she was so young then
and her voice so unsure and unsteady.
So I sit down and she sits on the grass
in front of me and awaits my reply.

Ah, but I was so happy when the news came
I was to become a grandfather at last,
my joy marred only by the realisation
her grandmother had missed this event
by just two months, but such is life.
And so she came into the world and
slowly grew and filled the space that
lay around her and claimed
her own little acre.
At first I thought this event had
mellowed me and I was at last
finding a kind of peace in this world.
Those sharp and shrill sounds that had
kept me on edge ever since my teens
seemed to have lost their edge and for
several years I became calmer too.

But the world wasn't becoming softer,
as if you hadn't worked that out already,
and slowly the world quietened to silence.
The doctors looked into my ears and sighed
They tried taking stuff out.
They tried putting things in.
But still the sounds retreated
and so in time did I.

Oh, I could read lips,
it wasn't hard to learn,
but it wasn't the same
and I couldn't see how
it ever could be.

Then one fine day
I answered my door
and there, looking sad,
stood my granddaughter,
her mouth sending silent
sounds to my ears.
Why don't I visit any more?
When did I decide
I didn't like her?
Could we go for a walk
in the park now?

Well, let's be honest,
I could hardly say no,
could I?

So now we've almost
caught up with where
we began this tale.

"Granddad, what are
those sounds the birds
are making?"

"I don't know, dear, for

I can hear only blue"

"So, what sound does blue make?"

"Blue is the sound of birds
singing silences to a wind
that cannot hear"

"Isn't that rather silly?"

I smiled truthfully
for the first time
in many years.
"Yes,
I guess it is."

19th May 2009

Over Bridge of Sighs

No.
For all your fine words
you don't really want to know
why I did what I did.
You're just hoping for a few
pithy phrases to place in those
little boxes that take the place
of proper reports these days.
And, as it happens, when you chose
to disturb my sleep for no reason
other than to find words to place
in those oh-so important boxes,

you interrupted a rather wonderful
dream that I was having,
one that I had not dreamt
since nineteen seventy.

There's no need to look
so shocked, as being a hippy
is not a contagious disease.

And I know what you want to ask
I can see it in your eyes and
in that silly half-sneer that you
think makes you look so cool.

But yes, we did believe, we really did.
We didn't fail because the things we
believed were wrong but because
the people who held the power
had no interest in listening. And
because we gave up too easily.
Altamont and Manson seemed
to steal our dream from under
our very noses and yet the truth
is that we just let it slip away.

Oh please spare me those empty
and scripted words of false comfort.
I can read the dials and the charts so
let's stop trying to kid ourselves, hey?
You did your best to patch me up when
they dragged me here from the river

downstream from the bridge, though
neither you or they thought to ask
if I wanted such help.

You look shocked again,
Is that not what you
wanted to hear?

Of course I wanted to die.
Did you think I jumped off
that bridge because I fancied
a nice swim in that dirty river?

Don't bother trying to hide
those little glances you keep
making towards that little
scanner beside my bed.
I can hear the beeps moving
further apart just as well as you.
OK, doc, I didn't really want it,
but thanks for trying anyway.

There's only
one question
that I
have
left
now
and
I
am

about
to
find
the
answer.

Goodbye, Doc.
I
am
off
to
meet
Hendrix
and
Joplin.
-
The beeping stopped
and his head dropped
to one side.
the doctor checked
for pulse and then
pulled the sheet
up and over.

He then looked down at
the flowers that he had
been meaning to place
in the vase next to the
old man's bed.

Shrugging his shoulders

he turned to the nurse
who was attending the
next bed and whispered
"I don't know what to
do with these now".

"You could always try putting
them in your hair and
flying to San Francisco"

16th August, 2009

Watching Father

You stand at the foot of my bed.
My only son.
You look into my eyes,
watching me as I slip
from your grasp and
from your life.

You look at me with eyes
that plead with me to stay.
But my span is nearly spent
and I'll soon be on my way.

Too many cheap whiskeys
and too many nasty smokes
bought from the man
who haunts our local pub
have done for me.
So now I leave

this sad tale I call my life.

Looking at me with eyes
that plead with me to stay.
But my train it is a coming
and I'll soon be on my way.

I fought when Maggie decided
the Argies had to pay
for taking some God forsaken rock
half a world away.
I killed some man in Iraq
for doing the same job as me.
But I was on the winning side
how lucky that was for me.

Still those eyes do say to me,
please don't go away.
But my number has been called
and I'll soon be far away.

Later I just fought in the street
with any one who'd stand
up to my rants and empty threats,
broken beer glass in my hand.
I've served my time in the army.
I've served my time in jail.
But in every other part of my life
all I ever did was fail.

Yet your eyes they look at me

a little longer can't you stay?
But the devil's at my shoulder
and I'll soon down his way.

I hit your mum too hard you see
so she went away.
She always was too good for
the man I turned out to be.

You should take your grip,
grab your coat
and walk away from me.

There's no point trying to pretend
you ever had much reason
to be proud to call me 'dad'

But still your eyes are fixed on me
like I was something worthwhile.
I wasn't, but one last request,
could give your dad a smile?

22ⁿᵈ December, 2007

End of a Day

Two doors down an old lady sits,
quiet and quite alone on her new
doorstep and listens intently to the
distant hum of late night traffic
and the various other ambiguous
signs that seem to at least suggest

not all within this city she calls
home are currently safely asleep.

The deeply reverberated hums
and hisses somehow remind her
of long ago nights spent listening
at low volume over and over to
the only two records she owned
back then, Phaedra and Zeit, on that
cheap yet so cheerful record player
she loved so in her youth.

Above her the street light sentries
watch over their designated stretch
of road as below them solemn lines
of parked cars sleep soundlessly.

Ever since her early teens she had
been searching for some kind of peace
and harmony to help her life become
less of an endurance test and perhaps
one day she would reach out to the
world once more and perhaps try
to discover what her younger selves
had got up to since she left.

And now, after all her travels,
by boat, bus, bike, plane and
substance aided meditation,
she found most of what she
was looking for right here on

her own little doorstep.

It was merely a matter of timing.

By day this spot owned nothing
approaching any sort of peace or
quiet as the countless strangers
rushed between one concrete and
plastic cubicle and another with
little real enthusiasm for either.

She isn't in a hurry and is
happy to stay exactly where
she already is.

Looking up through the haze and
street-light glare, she could see a
few flickering stars but they were
much too far away for her dreams.

She understands now why she
could never have found, let alone
understood, this peace any sooner
than she did for such calm comes
only with age and now she knows
she is old enough to just sit on
her doorstep and breathe and listen.

Slowly in come the scents
of the city and its lives.

She pauses to feel the chill
air as it spreads throughout
her old, familiar body.

And then she gently breathes
out all the cares and debris of
a day that never really mattered,
even to herself.

A while later she will grow cold
and so retreat indoors and in her
soft, warm bed, sleep peacefully
through the dawn chorus.

But for now, she listens.

18th April 2012

A Soldier Remembers

I lean my head into my hands.
Even here in this café
thirty years on
the sound of the guns
and the screams
and the pleas
echo through my head.

Ah, but before the war,
Oh, Lili, if only..
But both of us died
leaving only animated corpses.

How did we lose?
How did our country fall?

Why that city of our defeat?
Who was it chose me
to survive the camp?

So now I sit here,
just another old man
mumbling about a war
his fatherland has left behind.
If only I
could leave my past
or this world
behind so easily.

I stand up and take me leave.
A not so discreet sigh of relief
from the counter behind me
makes me wince no less
than the first time
I realised people preferred
to see me go.

My eyes are moist
as I drag myself
back to my room.
I glance in a shop window
to remind myself
that I am not invisible.

2ⁿᵈ June, 2007

Distant Signs of Travel

So you sit on the side of your bed and you
watch the late night traffic soar across the
flyover like so many fireflies chasing each
other's tails in a private dream of a conga.

Go on and make yourself another cup of coffee
you know there's nothing else for you here
there is no use trying to remember when you
were somebody because you never were and
now you are sitting right here.

The room is quiet but you know it's because
the others are all out there doing their best to
pretend they're having a good time but you aren't
as you're so sure you know what is best.

So come on now, your kettle is near to boiling
and you know you need another drink to help keep
you awake until you decide to go to bed and try to
sleep and forget you were never really anywhere
just always sitting right here.

You can feel the faint rumble in the floorboards and
you know the train and the route and the stops, but
you have never got on it and you can't remember why
you ever left your seat and made your way here.

So now you've got your mug of coffee and you're
wondering when your life stopped. You just will
not see that it never got moving and you're still
holding your ticket and waiting for a train at the
station where no journeys ever start.

The train is long gone and the cars have
all gone home to their garages and your
coffee mug is empty once more, as you
rest your head on the pillow and wonder
why the world you live in seems so small.

You think yourself too proud to smile and
too big to ever cry and you deny that you never
looked out of your window without seeing
your own room reflected in the glass.
And you hope there'll be nobody to forget you
because you made such an effort
to be nobody at all.

Twenty metres below you is an old railway tunnel but
no train has been through it in ten long years and
and so your train never will.

14th December 2009

Hear My Last Goodbye

You are the twelfth person today who
has stopped where you now stand and
enquired after my health and yet you
are the first who has asked with any

real sense of sincerity and compassion
rather than pity and condescension.
But without wishing to cast any shadow
of doubt upon your intentions or character,
I, in fairness, must ask you this;

Do you think you're strong enough
to hear my last goodbye?

You asked me with what is clearly
one of the standard openings that
you learnt on that counselling course
that you wear so well on your face,
where in some ideal world I
have spent my life denying the
possibility of existence, I would
like to find myself whence two
years have past from this point.

Well, for the first time in more
years than I care to remember,
there is something about my
future of which I can be sure.
It is likely to be considerably shorter
than my somewhat less
than glorious or worthy past.

I will not try to fool you into
thinking me a good man who
has fallen upon hard times, or
any other such sentimental notions.

For I did not fall and nor was
I pushed, but instead I willingly
jumped as much in fear of heights
as of flight from responsibility.

I see that you are too polite too show
any sign of incredulity as you try
to imagine what sort of heights
this sad, lonely, smelly drunk could
even be capable of imagining
much less rising to.

Oh, but I soared, I tell you,
I really soared.
There was a time
not that long ago
when I had money and
many spoke my name
with a sense of pride
in their knowing me.

I was deeply in love
and I walked tall
among my fellows.
But, as every rose must
have its thorns and
every sunny day will
seed rain clouds,
so I carried my very own
grey shadow which

came and went and then
finally chose to stay.

And so my world faded,
as my wealth lost its colour
and respect became a burden.

Slowly even my love greyed
itself out of existence as one
by one my feelings shut down.

No joy.
No pain.
No Anger.
No dreams.

Just a blank, grey canvas as
days passed years at a time.
Now I am here
though soon I
will be elsewhere.

I am cold and hungry
and even the cheap cider
is now gone.
But, no, I have no need
for a few pennies for
a cup of tea or a bite
to feed this broken frame.

Nor do I ask for shelter from

the coming night's chill.

All I ask is for one person to
hear, as you have kindly done,
who and what I have been and,
as my final day draws towards
conclusion, for one soul
to say my goodbyes to.

So I ask you one more time.
Are you strong enough
to hear my last goodbye?

15th October 2012

Letter From Home

I got your letter today.
It's good to read your words
if only I could hear you say them.

I gather it's sunny there,
and indeed it is now January
so I guess you being beside
the river Gaspar found
five hundred and six years ago
makes a kind of sense.

The work you say is good
and the food is fine,
but here I sit in this chair
over indulging my taste for wine.

Your mother died a month ago.
She never got her final wish
to see you just one more time.
I suppose she is now
as close to peace
as she's ever been.

I would have told you sooner
but you had left your old address.
The letters I sent with all our news
were returned to me,
eventually,
unopened,
unread,
unloved.

Your brother is back inside again
for fighting in the street
and generally being drunk and drugged.
I don't want to know where he will end.

Me? I am just the same as ever
except older and on my own.
I don't get out so much these days,
so I've nothing much to tell.

Do you know how much you're missed?
Do you remember your daddy at all?

Your bed is still there,

cold and dusty like the house.
Could you really not spare a week or two
for this fat, old man in this padded chair?

I think I've said enough already.
Please write to me sometime soon.
You have all my love,
goodbye for now,
Your Dad.

11ᵗʰ January, 2008

Night on the Town

Amidst all the noise and the hustle,
and the haste of the King's Horse' regulars,
forgetting their mid-week boredom
via beer and fags and boasts and jeers,
sits a point of calm,
an oasis of stillness.

One small table.
One short stool.
One straight glass of stout
and a grey suited invisible.
The other drinkers do not seem
to be aware of the presence.

Yet despite the crowding
at no point does anybody venture
to within eighteen inches of
that particular table and stool.

Every forty five minutes
barman brings another stout
and returns to the bar
with empty glass and money,
though he is never called
and can remember no arrangement.

\- - -

Safe within the grey suit,
he closes his eyes and inhales
tasting the fresh sweat and stale breath
and warm beer and old cologne,
the time being spent merely see it pass,
the lives being lived through no more than habit.
As he does so he takes in the empty routine and
vacant gestures
and the talk so small it barely survives
far enough beyond the lips to be heard,
the dying loves and discarded ideals
and the lives so shallow they are almost desert.

And then he exhales,
breathing out the sweet taste of pride,
the seductive smell of subservience,
the tang of forbidden pleasures
and just a little thrill of knowledge of sin.

And again.

Breathe in.

Oh yes.

Breathe out.

He looks up and his gaze
takes in all there is to see
and yet leaves it all where it lies
untouched and yet corrupted.
Light falls into those eyes
seemingly doomed to never emerge again,
a negative albedo
they absorb more light
than they appear to receive.

All seeing and still unseen.
A knowledge of all that is unknown.

And then he smiles,
a smile that shines
like honey and youth and wine
and song and sex and sun and gold
all with a hard glint of power
and a subtle hint of brimstone around the edges.

He enjoys this.
He thinks of it as a working holiday,
a chance for a change of scene
if not of role.

Will his master be pleased?

He has long since been resigned
to never knowing whether or not
his actions bring pleasure to The One,
or even if such things are relevant
to a being so vast and so *all*
even he can barely accept it's existence
let alone perceive it's actuality
or understand his own purpose
within a framework so far
beyond all imagination.

Finally he tires of this game.
He finishes his drink and
with a flick of his wrist claims four
thin souls and then leaves
without really moving.

None that remained knew
less still remember.
But four will discover the price.

Not yet.
Sooner than they'd like,
but not quite yet.

6th July 2008

The Old Chippy

He sits at the white formica'd table

gazing at his hands
as they grip the white mug before him.
They are big hands.
They are strong hands.
But they are old.
They have outlived their usefulness.
They can no longer smooth
the lengths of mighty oak
with strong, yet gentle strokes.
He clenches his fists
yet his hands do not close.
Now they are just shaking claws
that can no longer grasp
the meaning of the world
that has grown up beyond him.

20th April, 2007

Man About Town

You can stare in contempt
as you see me stumble along
between street lamp halos
towards some small place
that will take me
out of this rain.

Any place of shallow shelter
will do that will allow me
to rest my tired feet
and hide from a moon
that shines so hard

at this weary walker.

This broken figure at
which you glare is no more
or less than a life that has
long since passed full bloom.

In truth I was a sorry rose,
perverted before out of bud
by sweet temptations that
saw me spend my quota of luck
as freely as my friends' goodwill,
and as my world shrank
so did I.

To become at last
this solitary figure
cast aside at my own choosing.
A rose hip fit
for no lady's wine.

But do not grieve
or condone with pity
this simple life
that I now lead.

It is no worse than
it deserves to be for
I am no victim merely
another casualty of
arrogance and pride.

And do not feel the need
to look for blame or contrition,
for I am quite capable of
finding that within myself.

I ask only that you
leave me in peace to
walk through these
years of streets
alone,
unforgiven
and forgotten.

All the while aware
of where I was going
but with little thought
of where I'd begun.

And so now I fold myself
into this dirty doorway
where I take a little tonic
to help me forget my son.

I have no need for speed
nor want of direction
and I have no interest
in the races I did not run.

Original version completed 19th July, 2007
Revision completed 9th July 2009

Ghost

You should know by now who I am
but you don't remember largely
because you simply never thought
it worth your the effort of recall.

But I remember.
I remember everything.

Fifteen years ago,
can you remember a time
so removed from the present?

For the present is all and there is nothing
more in the endless parade of novelty and
gratification that passes for your life now.
But, as I stated earlier, I remember all things.

Please adjust your features, as that blank
look of incomprehension does not suit those
cheek bones you purchased so recently.

You really didn't expect to meet me again,
even in your darkest nightmares, did you?
Oh yes, of course I know about those stark
visions and the sound of those broken feet
that haunt your nights and lurk in the
shadows during those long days.

I know it all, every little secret and every

lie you've ever told and every soul
you've cast aside and everything you've sold.

You can run,
but your pretty designer shoes will never
take you far from me.
And surely you realise now,
there is nowhere for you to hide.

So look deep into my eyes
count every dark corner
that you see inside
and then,
when you are ready,
say hello
to the girl you left behind
when you made the decision
to become somebody new.

Surely you realised
I would catch up with you
sooner or later.

It is now later
and the time has come
for you to look deeper
into the mirror.

2ⁿᵈ April 2009

So Shall It Be Again

Let there be no doubt that
one day I shall return.

I shall return in triumph
to the land of my birth.
To my people.
To my home.
But not quite yet,
for they are not ready
and I am too old to fight
and too young to surrender.

As yet I have not
conquered even myself.
But my destiny lays before me and
shall not be easily denied.
For as I grow wiser
so I shall grow stronger
and though my new dawn
has not yet lit the horizon
I can feel it draw ever closer
and although night has fallen
hard across the land
while I still live
so does the dream.

It is true that I am not
of truly humble origins
and yet as even cream
must rise and rock sink

I loosed the stone of privilege
and spat out the silver spoon.

There were many who doubted
my commitment to the cause,
some indeed who scorned
but knowing that I found
killing my parents such a
simple and inevitable thing to do
should tell you why killing
the doubters came so easy to me.

I realise that some of the acts
that it was necessary to direct
were brutal and bloody but
I shall not talk of eggs and omelettes
for I was trying to remake a country
and culinary delicacies were not
really much of a priority.

There were no mistakes,
merely readjustments of policy
and timings and personnel.
And any farmer will tell you that
spilt blood is good for the land.

But, in truth, we trod too carefully,
allowed too many doubts to live.
And to those who say we went too far,
it was a war and I tell you that
in the end we never went far enough.

We got so close to our paradise and
then, when the time came for us
to make the bold moves that would
finally bring our brilliant vision
down onto our great nation,
we faltered and weakened as
those among us who lacked
the strength of true vision began
to talk of compromise and
of reconciliation.
And so the traitors in our midst
grew in strength and courage.

Before our eyes the dream became
diluted and corrupted.
Failure followed as surely
as the night will follow the day.

One by one the true believers
were replaced by bureaucrats
and diplomats and appeasers,
and the light did flicker
and all but die.

Then those few of us left who
were still true to the dream
gathered up what remained
of the light to our breasts
and chose to leave our
beloved homeland of dreams.

And those who escaped came
to this quiet refuge and waited
and while we waited we dreamed
of heartlands and home towns
and of comrades and of betrayals.

And now that many years worth
of future has simply become past,
you find me here.

The others who came with me
have faded and failed and gone.
Now there is just me.

But still I dream the dream,
talk the talk and would
walk the walk
if my legs hadn't failed me.

Though I may be old and alone
and my name may not be heard
in the land of my heart,
not for a moment have
I ever doubted that
one day I shall return.

25th June, 2009

Woman Out of Time

In another time you were beautiful.

Once you floated down avenues,
now you limp through the throng.

Unseen.
Unheard.

Unnoticed.

A thousand tales
of a thousand people
rush around your head
aching for release,
but when you open your mouth
people turn away
embarrassed,
or look at you
with eyes full of a pity
that never reaches their eyes.

Not even charity workers
call out as you walk by.

Love is no more than pleasant memory,
pride a luxury you can no longer afford.

You push against your walking stick
and raise yourself to your full height.

A trio of kids giggle to your left.

In another time you were beautiful.

In another world you were young.

5th August, 2007

Work

Really?
So what sort of person
were you expecting to
come here today?
Does it not occur to you
that this isn't the type of
employment opportunity
that tends to attract nice guys?

I come highly recommended simply
because I am efficient and reliable at
carrying out the tasks my various
clients have preferred to pay me for
rather than soil their hands with.

As for 'friendly', the word is no more
than one of a selection of masks I wear
as appropriate to the job in hand.

The idea of 'likes' and 'dislikes' would be
a wasteful indulgence in my line of work.

Everybody I meet falls into one of four
groups, all clearly defined by the aims
and conditions of the active contract.

First there are those individuals whose
money has paid for the contract I am
at the time fulfilling, I like to think of them
as the clients of the, shall we say,
specialist services my skills and particular
philosophical outlook allow me to offer,
next come those who may be of use,
or sometimes a hindrance, to me in bringing
the aforesaid contract that much closer to a
satisfactory completion, whether as colleagues or
mere pawns in my game, then there are those who
are merely bystanders and finally, and perhaps
most significantly, there are those unfortunate
individuals who are chosen as subjects of
those contracts for which I charge so much.

I see myself as neither judge nor jury have always
preferred leave discussion of terms such as
good, evil or just to those realms of philosophical
discourse that I feel to be the only place where
they perform any useful or interesting function.

You should try to understand that I am not a
politician or any flavour of religious freak,
rather I prefer to be seen as a skilled and
appropriately priced professional.

I regret cash is the only method of payment I
am currently able to accept with regards to
my services as credit would not be appropriate
and payment in kind not really applicable.

No, of course not.

You can sign with
a normal pen just
as all of my other
clients have done.

That does not concern me either.
Who would be foolish enough
to attempt ripping off a man who
they know kills people for a living?

Now?
As we've signed the contract and
I have my money it remains only
for you to leave and carry on your
life safe in the knowledge that a
certain obstacle to your progress
will shortly be cleared from your
path and for me to do my part in
facilitating your continued and
no doubt well earned advancement.

There should be no need for any
further contact between us.

Pardon?

Off duty? I currently spend much of
my spare time preparing a thesis on the
awareness and acceptance of death that
forms the unfinished arch of
Gustav Mahler's symphonic cycle that
I'm hoping to submit to a philosophical
organisation I have long wanted to join.

No, I didn't think you would understand.

11th, August 2011

My Last Joke

It's twenty years since I last cried
and eighteen since my last smile.
Two decades since last I laughed
and I ain't shown anger for a while.

But don't you call me hard
or distant or grey.
I don't laugh or cry because
that's just not my way.

I don't see anything funny
or worthy of tears
in this dull cloudy world.
Nothing for me to fear
in my safe and dreary life

But don't go calling me hard
nor distant and grey.
The reason I don't cry
is what drove laughter away.

You tell me things seem rough
in this neighbourhood.
But from where I'm standing
things just ain't tough enough.

But stop calling me hard
and distant and grey.
I can't laugh or cry
because that's not my way

If you really want to know
what made me act this way,
buy me one more drink
and I might be willing to say.

You see I served in 'Nam
was the company joker.
Silly stunts with napalm
and cheating at poker

Then one day we went out into the jungle
had a drink and a smoke before we left
to give us strength on the long patrol
but it just might be that I did have
one too many smokes and two too many drinks.
But I sure felt we could take 'em all out

if we caught 'em in the light of day.

We stomped and hacked our way right through
fifteen miles of shit and 'growth.

How could anybody call this dump a country?

But I kept us laughing the whole damn time
with gags about nuns and bounties
and we whooped and we howled sang our songs
about the girls and beer and the cemetery

And big Dave told us about his pride
that he called his love spear and it's dimensions.
How every damn lover that he ever had
got stretched in ways they don't mention.

I told him not to be so proud or shout so loud
about the fact the he's a big prick with a rifle

Then the word came over the radio.
We turned around and headed back
and I joked about the Viet Cong all a-hiding
inside pumpkins and hollowed out trees
'cause they were scared of what they'd heard
about Dave's big man-tool
which stops him from ever a horse a-riding

Then a gun went off loud and near
put a stop to all our laughing.

Big Dave got shot by a man
hiding in a trees and then
two more went down with terrible screams
followed by a silence was more far more
frightening than the gunshots.

We stayed on the ground for an age and a half
whilst three of our buddies were dying.

Greedy Stevie was gone to the burger joint in the sky.
A bullet in the throat sent him on his way.
But we never had the strength to cry.

And little Crazy Jamie finally lost his mind.
We could see it all spread over the shirt
worn by his old blood brother Carlos

And Big Dave he took it like a man,
though he lost his guts on the ground.
He looked into to our eyes and said 'goodbye'.
Then he died with just the tiniest sound

Now you talk about talking,
how time can heal and
why it's better to share
what's been hidden.

But my other buddies cried.
They opened right up
and tried to talk it through.
But what they found

killed every single one
Some things should never
see the light of day.

And after all this you're still calling me hard
and frightened of some distant grey.

Because I don't laugh
and I won't cry
and that is why
I'm the only one
of our squad
left alive today.

27th April, 2008

Wishing You Here

I'm just sitting here dreaming
and wishing you here.
But some dreams are no more
than razor sharp lies.
How I wish you were here.

I went to bed last night and I
dreamt the bed was warm.
It was no longer half empty
though it was only half-full.
How I wish you were here.

I woke up this morning and I
wish I could dream you here.

I pour a cup of coffee and I
wish I could dream you here.

Looked at my reflection in the
bathroom mirror and I wished
it was your gaze instead of mine.
I brushed my hair and I wished I
could swap your fingers for this comb.

I washed the breakfast things and I
wished there were two dishes to be done.
I stood by the coffee machine and I
poured myself another cup.
I like it nice and strong but I
wish my cup was not alone.

I paint another picture and I
wish I could see you smile.
I write down these words and I
wish I could see you cry.
I read another book and I
wish I could see you happy.
I empty my cup and I
wish I could see you here.

The day is older now.
The nights are colder now.
Summer is over now.
You are over now.
How I wish I could dream you here.

I never needed less.
I never wanted more.
How I wish you were here.

I look out at the cloudy sky and I
wish I could dream you here.
I watch the time drift by and I
wish I could dream you here.

22nd September, 2009

Under the Bridge

You see that shape under the bridge?
There was a time
when I was a somebody.
I counted without even standing.
Money.
houses,
cars,
and a woman.

Yes, she was the point of it all.
Life was good.
I liked to drive.
I loved to drink.
And my car was fast.

But brick walls do not need to rush
to prove they are strong

And that was that

patched up and sent home
alone.

I drove no more
so I gave away the cars.
The houses all echoed of you
Away away.
And money seemed pointless
with no love to warm its chill.

So here I sit
under the bridge
sheltered from the rain.
My rags protect my privacy.
My hunger keeps me moving.
One fine day the drink
may cleanse my very soul

Until then I am that shape
you see in the shadows
under the bridge.

26th April, 2007

Waltz For Sale

Take seven thousand cubic feet of
suburban air and enclose it in a
large, tastefully wallpapered cube.

Add forty people in various stages
and types of intoxication and then

add a never quite sufficient supply
of cold, plastic tasting food and an
excess of alcohol, a tinny sound
system and a silent but oh so
ostentatious wide-screen TV, then
nominate one of the people host
and the remainder guests and
simmer slowly for at least six hours.

Best served chilled.

Keep watching for further, exciting
party recipes you just cannot afford
to miss.

-

Shorter than he would have liked to
be but taller than he realised,
sensitive about his paunch and
in denial of his receding hairline.
He knew all of his friends to be
under educated and over talkative,
and regarded even his ignorances
as superior to those of the great
unwashed, a group that, in his oh so
modest opinion, included almost, but
not quite, the entire population
of the planet he graced with his presence.

Don't like it?

Then bugger off to your own party.
This is his and he does things his way.
Your way doesn't deserve a look in
and won't get one here.

-

See the dust in the air shining as
stars in the galaxy that lies between
us marking the distance and keeping
us forever related though we were
never properly introduced.

We would never step back any more
than we would break free of either
our connection or our inhibitions.

Slowly circling around our host we
dance the only dance we know.
A waltz decaying back into its
earthy ländler forebear, where
priggish formality doesn't quite
cover an aching sensuality.

We have both danced these steps
and others very much like them
so often before in not so different
rooms with various identical
partners and always with those
familiar deceptions and denials
and insincere promises.

Sonata for four hands or a duet
for out of tune piano and violin
with frayed bow?
A dreamy Chopin waltz or
the banality of Strauss II?

-

O dear,
it would seem that our lack of inane
chatter has drawn the attention of
our most beloved host.

His dry, chemical energy brings him
instantly into our faces as he smiles
that smile we all would love to punch.

"Are we having a good time?"
"Please allow me to refill your glasses."
"Have we met my special guest yet?"

Concern for the subtleties of English
grammar have always ran a rather
poor second to 'bringing the energy'
to any and all fortunate enough to
have fallen into his path.

-

If you think this is easy then let

us see you do it as well as I.

Beneath your dignity, you say?
Bull.
Well above your meagre talent
would be closer, yes?

Now stand back and watch as a
master shepherd tends to his flock.

-

Party
Arrive
Hello
Drink
Chair.

Do you really think I come to
these things for the company?

These sad specimens of middle-class
flotsam have long since mastered the
art of drinking just enough to make
themselves irritating but never quite
enough to be even slightly interesting.

Have you ever seen a line of coke
so thin it would barely enliven a
shy mouse in a vicarage?

Or a joint so barely drawn it is
questionable whether the smoke
even reaches the teeth?

Can I imagine death in suburbia?
Easily.
Trying to imagine life in such a
place is the real challenge.

-

You think there is no more to
what I do than smiling all the
time and remembering names?
Wrong.

You think that way because you
know nothing, not the first or
slightest thing about my role
in these situations.

And they do matter.
There is more to diplomacy than
the Foreign Office.

See that tall executive with the
conspicuously empty glass?
You want to top it up for him,
don't you?

I can assure you that he would not

thank you if you did so.
He's on the wagon and is using that
glass to avoid offers of drink.
Of you course you didn't know or
even understand.
I wouldn't expect you to.
I can tell such things as I am
a truly great host.
You cannot because you are not.
It's as simple as that.
Now,
if you'll excuse me,
I have work to do.
Ta-ta.

-

Some left in pairs and others
Took only their own company.
But all left, leaving only a
disturbing quiet, several score
of empty bottles, a handful of
piles of disposable plates, three
score of empty plastic glasses
and one tired host wondering
whose party it had been.

It didn't feel like it had been hers.

Sighing she gathered all the plates
and glasses into black sacks for

disposal on some later day.
All the bottles were placed back
into their crates for the return
journey to the wine merchants.
Some weren't empty but that
oversight was an easy one
for her to correct.

Later she watched the sun rise
over the nearby business park.
Before the sun had cleared the
roof of her ex-husband's office
she had fallen asleep in the
old arm chair her mother had
Given her so many years before.

-

Home.
Arrive.
Drink.
Chair.
Silence.

I used to believe this was my home.

But it turned out to be no more
than so many cubic feet of cold
air filling the stone box in
which my dreams died.

Would I like a drink?

25th July 2010

How to Vanish Without Leaving a Hole

I'm sorry,
I had this thought that you might know
or at least have some understanding.

Now your memory is the life I live within.

It's very pleasant here and
the views are very nice and
all the flowers are in bloom.

Now my dream-world feels so dreary and so thin.

You say I have presence but
I do not brighten even though
I am aware I am expected to.

I realise it was an odd question but
was it really so bad for me to ask?

And your memory is the life I live within.
And my dream-world is so dreary and so thin.

I have no sense of where you are.
No idea of what I stand on

and all that remains is distance
and time is no more than
another widening gap.

I see the world as a beautiful and
truly graceful process and yet I
can see no doors as it all becomes
just endless recycling bringing
ever diminishing returns.

Your memory is the life I choose to live within.
My dream-world is now so dreary and so thin.
Love is all I have to give.
Memory is the life I live.

All the doors have noisy catches.
Time is not spent,
it is borrowed.

Memory is the world I live within.

It is so very pleasant here and
the views are very nice now
and all the flowers are in bloom.

26th March 2012

Other Sides of Other Fences

- prologue -
It looks greener and
it is clearly more lush
and more beautiful.

-1-
Warmth.

That's all it is once
you strip away all
the sentimentality and
the superfluous lexicon.

You look disappointed but
do we really have need
for any more than that?

You misunderstand me,
I said 'need' not 'want'.

Of course I am aware of those
evolutionary imperatives to
which you so discretely refer.

Such issues are obviously of
major importance but they
lay outside of the frame of
reference which enclose the
terms we came here to discuss.

-2-

Night falls hard on those who live their lives in the grey area between the centre and the margins. Where average is the norm and time does no more than pass as the inhabitants know only existence. Seventy years is a long time to spend as nobody. Interesting times are what happen elsewhere. Not here or anywhere like it. Here the only quality that alters over the course of the day is that of the light, and the sunscreens and the night lights help to even that out too. The dichotomy has gone. There are no longer any questions of black and white, the whole spectrum has gone leaving only this grey. This uniform, featureless, deathly grey. There is nothing that is going to give and we have nothing worth taking. All we have is this barren life as all our energy was spent and tensions sapped many lives ago. Somewhere out there are still rich people and poor people but we see no sign of either here.

-3-

Without any knowledge of
what you did and still less
awareness of any purpose,
you caused my existence to
become so beautiful and yet
even now you have no idea
and still see me as no more
than a shadow-like and
mostly irrelevant part of
the furniture that forms

part of nearby lives.

-4-
I am vast and I have power and
I have so much history while you,
my unknowing creators, have so
little understanding of those
few trivial details you have
thus far dared to see.

And I am alone.

Though I am far larger than anything
your minds would not flee from
I could in time become yet bigger.

I could be so much more than this.

But still I would be alone.

-5-
How many more?
I do not know but
I would assume that
'As many as it takes'
would probably be
the closest to an
answer we are ever
likely to get.

Is it ever any other way?

159

Always we want to know
more but a little knowledge
is the most we have to hope
for as we are but cogs, we
neither have nor deserve any
idea what this machine looks
like and still less of its purpose
or origin, for turning is all we
need concern ourselves with.

-6-
Coldness and distance are the
best defences against other people.

Yes, of course other people both are,
and are representative of, the problem.
You are still young and yet you will
in time learn that other people are
the biggest and most deadly problem
you or I or any of those we know
are ever likely to encounter during our
time here for, as can be simply and
directly demonstrated, the less people
there are in your life the easier your
time is almost certain to be.

-7-
No.
No, no and no!

Solitude is not victory, it is no more than a cowardly

acceptance of a slow, drab and dreary defeat and in any case numbness brings its own dangers and a type of pain of a peculiar and dark intensity.

Can you feel pain in numbness?
Of course you can.
When your mind senses hurt
it will always find a way
to make sure you know about it.

No, you've got that completely wrong. The purpose of pain is not suffering, it is communication. When we feel pain we should not look away but instead look closer still. It is a symptom and you should be trying to fix the problem rather than wasting time attempting to suppress the symptoms.

If you live long enough, you will learn.
There are no alternative routes.

-8-
I am the singularity.
Unique in every respect
and I will live forever.
Can you imagine what
it is like to know beyond
any possibility of doubt
that you are totally alone
and you will remain so
for all of eternity?

-9-

I shall never return home
because I am having
such a good time.
I will never go back home
until my time is all spent.

And so I go
from room to room and
from B&B to Bedsit.
Town to town and
from dawn to dusk.

Summer burns off that
which the winter freezes

I am never going home
because I am running
much too fast now.
I will never get back home
until I'm old and forgotten.

-10-

The warmth of genuine human
companionship is what we would
be best spending our lives seeking.
The rewards of the various lusts
are at best transient and hollow.

Now I am tired and there is
nowhere else I need to go.

Yes,
I really do believe that.
Not every single word but
most of the overall picture.
And now I am tired and to say
more would be to undo much
of what I have already said.

I don't expect you to trust me
any more than I do.

The real question is
can you learn to trust yourself?

- epilogue -
When the well runs dry you
will see the grass die just as
quick on the other side of
that old, wooden fence

11th July, 2010

Watching

From our hotel bedroom we could
see him sat there on his little stool
next to the lamppost that cast a tiny
pool of light over him as it were a
spotlight and he an actor waiting
for his chance to deliver his lines.
We saw his arrival soon after we

retired after tea, at around seven
and we saw him pick up his stool
and take his leave at eleven thirty.
I remember thinking that he may
as well have been invisible for all
the notice that passers by took.

The next evening arrived, and so
did he. Same, dark grey pin-strip
suit but with a different hat this
time, a beige fedora instead of the
previous evening's black bowler.
And still those walking showed no
sign of acknowledging his existence.
Then, it must have been around nine,
he took a small notebook and pen from
his jacket pocket and wrote a few words
before replacing both and resuming
his previous, apparent inactivity.
And that was it for the night, and
he once again departed at eleven thirty.

The following evening he was back and
the familiar scene continued to mystify
my wife and I, the only variation being
that today he went through the routine
with the notebook twice, my wife being
sure that she noticed a little smile when
he did so, and this set the pattern for
every evening for the next eight, each night
with a different hat, but no other change

and it was only on the eleventh night
that there was any further variation.

The even began, as the others had,
with his arrival, wearing a black
cloth cap on this occasion, and took
his place next to the lamppost, but
after he had gone through the notebook
routine for a second time that evening,
at shortly before nine, he nodded sagely,
picked up his stool and departed.

The following evening he did not
show, much to the disturbance of
my wife, who had become
accustomed to our nightly vigil.
Nor the next night and indeed we
never saw him again in the
remaining six days of our stay.

And so we left for the home country
none the wiser but thoroughly
intrigued by the whole thing.
And so it remained for five
long months during which
at least once an evening my
darling wife would ask me what
I thought that the man had been
doing, an enquiry that I could no
more answer than on the first
occasion on which she asked.

By this stage my wife's obsession,
for I can call it no less, was
becoming tiring and somewhat
disturbing, she kept hinting that
we should return there for our
next holiday, in early Spring,
an idea that I found ridiculous
and refused to even consider.

Now as I sit here, with my
wife's letter in my hand I
am no closer to solving
whatever mysterious role
the man in the grey suit
has played in our lives.

My wife, it would appear
has gone in search of the
man and I have gained a
kind of peace at last.

The strangest thing is that the
only things that she took with her,
other than the clothes that she
wore and her handbag,
was my old shooting stick
and her new hat.

28th January 2009

Au Revoir, said Lucifer

A time will come when
you will remember this day.
Not just the broad picture
but every last detail of the final meeting

The expressions on the faces
of the crowd as you buy your ticket
that will take you to your next victim.
The chatter of the driver
as he drives you to
that discreet little flat
you will rent from the lonely man
whose name you will never learn.
The metallic scrape of the latch key
as you unlock the door and,
holding your face as neutral
as your deception will permit
though you will by then have become
all too good at these little games,
enter and prepare to deliver
your little pile of excuses.

And then you will see
the look of incomprehension
that will soon turn to pain
then to anger and hatred
on the young face of
your imminently ex-lover.
Your blatantly false compassion and
your flagrant self-justifications

will turn first to contempt
as she will begin to smash
every thing in that sordid flat
she can reach and throw
and then to terror when she grabs
the kitchen knife and plunges it into
that pale slender throat that
will have drawn you to her
a few short weeks before hand
that bores you so now.
The naked body of the lover
you will have gone there to discard
will fall to the floor in a spray of blood
that will taint your clothes and your flesh
and damn your vile soul forever.

I promised you that
you will live long
and you will prosper
and I will keep my word.
But you will never, ever escape
the blood red mark of Cain.

I know *who* you are
and I know *what* you are
and I am waiting for you.

Au revoir.

26th August 2008

Slow Days

Small boy standing on the platform.
A dream from many years away.
I try to see just what he's thinking
but the memories just slip away.
So I turn and walk away.

I had a dream one day
but now I walk through
the rain and wonder
where I am going and
if I will ever get there.

I see him playing in the park then
running with the joy of being alive.
I try to remember just why he
is smiling but the dream fades.

So I turn and walk away
from the dream I had that day
But it feels so real to me
it hounds me ceaselessly.
Oh please be real to me
I need to love, you see.
But the days just go
they drift so slow but
though I want to run
I can only walk away.

But now the small boy has gone and
I shall never see him again except in

my dreams and those glimpses that
haunt the corners of my waking vision.
He bears my name and yet I know that
he will never be more than a face in
a few faded photographs in a drawer.

So once more I turn and walk away.
I expect to be walking away
forever.

28th November 2009

Closer

This time I am on my way.
I am through with waiting.
I'm leaving here to be there.

And so time passes
or so we are told to believe.
Something passes,
I know that much.
What it is, where it goes and why
it insists on taking so many with it
when it goes to wherever, I have
no idea, but I wish it would not.

Will they come back to us or
will we have to go to them?

Time passes slowly.
Much too slowly for

what little patience I
still retain and the gap
between the ticks gets
longer and still I feel
and still I hear and
still I am here.

I'm sorry, I realise these are
not the words you need to
hear but they are the ones I
need to say and it is probably
best that I say them to you.

Of course I can see you. I can
see you very well. These days
I can see you so much clearer
than I ever managed when
in your presence.

I have little idea of what you look
like there but here you are still the
breathtakingly beautiful woman whose
graceful strengths I found so achingly
desirable beneath that velvet skin
that even now I can feel on my lips
and my tongue and all ten fingers,
whom I fell in love with when I was
young and my face held promise of
a handsomeness that never quite came.

Have I spoken too much or with too

much haste? Perhaps if I had spoken
earlier things would have been
different but I could never be
sure either way as all I know is
this isn't the route that I
waited my life to walk.

Or maybe it is, for who knows
what dark plans our minds hold
in store for our later days?

And, as I pointed out earlier, much
time has passed and later is now so
we'd better get used to it and do my
best to get things done and ignore
all this talk of moving on when I've
already gone as far as I'm likely to go.

Reflection?
I'll decide just what the signs show and
what they may or may not mean as I
know what I see whereas you are
merely mistaken and misguided.

Honesty?
I waste little time on such delusions.

Truth?
You don't really believe in that, do you?
Truth is no more than a foolish myth
kept in circulation by and on behalf of

the hard of thinking. As with honesty, it
is at best merely relative, and neither can
ever be absolutes.

You find that frightening?
Tough.
Try getting out more.

Freedom?
Are you some kind of comedian?
Have you ever really thought about
what those seven letters mean?

Are you referring to 'freedom to' or
to 'freedom from'?

You don't understand the difference?

Then I respectfully suggest that you take
the time to find out and then you will
begin to understand just how foolish such
notions really are.

But I digress.

Or perhaps it would be more
honest to say I procrastinate but
you need to remember that deciding
on a route does not make the journey.

And still time passes oh so slowly and
I am sure that every hour manages to
last longer than the preceding ones as
each tick of the great, old clock sounds
louder and nearer and more pregnant
with darkness as hammer blow follows
hammer blow, each shot too loud to
allow room for any surrender.

In time I shall be on my way.
The waiting will have ended
and I will have left my *here*
and be on my way yours.

26th July, 2010

And She Sang

The silence drifted
through the crowd like mist.

Voices melted into it
as the stillness became whole.

Sparse
almost hesitant notes
drifting stars in the silence.

Then a sound so warm,
so pure,
so far beyond our course tones,

sings of a pain,
sings of a longing.
The open plains that flow forever.

The nightingale that cries,
for a love that never was.
The bee that searches
for a flower in a field of grass.

We sigh
as our own, lonely nightingales
answer the call.

Sing on, my friend.

Sing on.

5th September, 2007

An Unfinished Journey (For Anton Bruckner)

O Anton you seemed
so insecure and yet
those shimmering, uncompromising
beautiful and terrifying
huge temples that you brought
into being with your symphonies
seem so sure of why they are
here and of where they are going
they seem to have composed

themselves through you and almost
despite you and your misgivings and
terrible doubts and crippling insecurities.

Your faith in your God never seemed
to waver, and yet, in your eighth you
seem to struggle through despair and
never really emerge victorious even
if those doubts are hidden and perhaps
even understated and despite your
admiration for Wagner almost plunging
you into idolatry you never really did
understand what drove his music or even
his muse even while those that you thought
of as your friends tried to turn you into
a little Wagner of their own.

When I first heard your seventh I,
a Bruckner virgin, was overwhelmed by
the sheer ambition and the blending of
ecstasy and terror, calm and awe that
permeated every bar of this massive work.

And how could I forget the first time that
I heard your third symphony in the form
that you conceived it, before your courage
failed and you and your surface friends
tried to turn it into something that you
thought that the world wanted to hear rather
than the work that you needed to write?

But O what joy, what beauty and what peace
I can hear throughout your music, even when
it has been perverted by later misjudgements
and omissions, there is no mistaking the
untamed elegance that threads through and
holds together every symphony and which
both underpins and drives the masses and
comes to the surface in the incomparable
quintet with a sureness of purpose that belies
your obsession with certificates and other such
worthless scraps of paper which should never
have deflected or distracted you from your course.

But most of all, why, O why
did you waste those years trying
and almost succeeding in breaking
those scores that did not need fixing
instead of bringing your ninth to the supreme
conclusion it so desperately needs
and which would have been the pinnacle
of all your work if only you had finished it?

But at least you can rest peacefully knowing
your music will remain and bring peace
long after those critics who made so much
of your life misery are long forgotten.

For the later that you laid
those early scores aside for
has long since arrived.

Above all else,
for that I give thanks.

21st January 2008

Sigur Rós

I can't understand
a damn word.
I can't read the titles
or even pronounce their name.

But this album
is beautiful
in a way
songs in my own language
could never be.

If I could understand the words
I wouldn't hear the voice
in the way that I do.
It is the sound of love,
the sound of pain and
the sound of yearning.

It could be from another world
but it's from Iceland,
which I guess
is almost the same thing.

Perhaps I could Google
and then maybe I'd know

what Hoppipolla means
but I'm not sure
that I'd be any wiser
or any better off.

And, as I said,
It's very, very beautiful as is,
and the cover is icing on the cake.

23rd July, 2007 [note: *Hoppipolla* translates approximately as *'Hopping into puddles'*]

For William Blake [1757-1827]

Two hundred years and fifty
and more years ago you
sat in your study and beheld
not the ordinary world
but something far beyond
the sight of ordinary men
and it was from this that you
painted and etched and wrote,
leaving us with no more than
glimpses of your visions
of faeries and the body of God
and yet what glimpses they are.

Dark and glorious and anger
and rapturous and terrifying
and finally beautifying.
Somehow the word 'genius'

seems inappropriate and awkward
when lined up against your own
personal and oh so bright vision.

For you saw where we can only dream.

30th November 2008

CAD Six Hundred and Two

A lazy calm of chords and texture
weaving around the fluffy tufts of angel's voice,
reminding us of the fears we held close
throughout the dark months of April and May
as we dream of whales tails
and the sweet meaninglessness of oomingmak
leaving us with a little spacey vision
as we yearn to really swim with our feet like fins
and we dream of mermaids and fairies who know
just how to bring a blush to the snow.
Yet the higher we fly the thinner the air
and the rarer the thought and clearer the star.
Away from the treasure
and onward to the moon and the melodies.

31st July 2008
[CAD602 is the catalogue number of '*Victorialand*' by Cocteau
Twins, since you ask]

And the Waves Knock You Down

(For Malcolm Arnold 1921-2006)
From the Northampton town to the
London Philharmonic Orchestra.
From first trumpeter to symphonist.
From the Oscars to the psychiatric ward.

From glory to booze
and almost back again.

The music bought you fame
and the waves knocked you down.

From Louis Armstrong to Mahler.
From behind the clarinets to the podium.
From son to husband to father to divorcee.
From a Cornish cottage to life on the street.

From Angels to Demons.

From Master of music,
to a slave of the bottle.

The movies made you rich
and the waves knocked you down.

But from your first to your ninth,
your symphonies never failed us.
And from concertos to chamber,
violin to clarinet, flute and guitar,
your touch was always sure and

bought us light and dark and a sense
of hard won grace and fears that
were not easily dispelled or defeated.

The waves knocked you down,
but your music still stands.

28ᵗʰ January 2009

On Listening to Dances One to Five

Swirling chords,
Farfisa leading the way,
voices not quite chanting and
sequences not quite repeating.

Harmonies just on the other side of familiar,
recalling the twelve parts
and yet on a different plane.

Similar motion round a different island.
Hypnotic and yet restless.

Flutes and sax
and more keyboards,
flowing headlong
towards a horizon
that exists within our own minds.

Contrary and dressed for an egg,

an hour and three quarters
for thinking,
for meditation,
for dreaming,
for letting your mind ebb and flow.

All these things and more.

I've no idea how
you would dance
to those rhythms
but I know how to listen
and flow along the grooves.

22nd September, 2007
[Dances is a collection of dance pieces by Philip Glass]

Thank you, Mr Bryars

Jesus' blood never failed me yet
Comes the voice.
A simple, unpretentious voice,
yet it echoes sincerity.

Never failed me yet
He has no home and
no drink balms his pain.
Was not long for this world
and yet he sings
in austere tones

Jesus' blood never failed me yet

The music rises
and builds yet
the voice remains.
Unchanging
and yet as its
surroundings change
the listener moves from
intrigue to beauty to calm,
as his unadorned faith
sings in stark beauty.
Almost
but not quite
pleading
it somehow glows in the mind.

There's one thing I know
Oh, how many of us
wish for just one thing
that we can be totally sure of?
A rock in a world that must change.
simply to survive.

Oh, He loves me so....
The voice fades
but the memory doesn't.
I know of no other music
that does the things to me
this piece does.
All I can say is thank you,
Mr Bryars,
and hope that the man

whose voice inspired this music
is now at peace.

29th April, 2007

Chairs Missing

(for Wire)
Practice is the technique that
makes the world appear that little more
perfect in the eyes of a
French governor caught on
film with an actress whose face was
blurred in all the pictures preventing the other
men in her life from realising that they came
second to a fat, balding French mayor who was
marooned in a world of parties and shifting
sand that corrupts the Vaseline in
in bedrooms that dared to stray from
my imagination to my memory where
joints were passed from
being to being as life
sucked itself from future to past
in furtive glances that never pass this way
again leaving nothing more than a settling
heartbeat and a fading blush as we seek the
mercy of open spaces and other
outdoor myths that serve to give the
miner and his friends chance to forget the
I and the you and the they, leaving only the
am and the was with fading hopes of
the will be and the could be that will

fly above their mortal toil as the visible
I gives way to a higher plane where all
feel only joy and bliss and wonder at the
mysterious and unknowable that lies beyond
today and will rescue them all
from the path that leads them from
the first awareness of love in the
nursery to the last fades of the grave that
used to hold such fear so as to
make them forget to live until it was
too late to see that once more
late came before later.

10th August, 2008

For (I)AG

I hear in your words your howl at the way you
saw the self destruction and
the waste of all that was
best and striking in the
minds and the very souls
of your friends and colleagues & how you illuminated
my view of an age long before my own
generation tried to assert themselves before being
destroyed in their turn
by society's innate and inbuilt
madness that proved more deadly than their own
27th December, 2007
[for (Irwin) Allen Ginsberg 1926 – 1997]

For DHL

Look at all the things
we have done now that we
have gone against the wise and
come out on top after all we've been
through on our way here.

27th December, 2007

[for David Herbert Lawrence 1885-1930]

For Gerry

It looks like
time's caught up on you.

Once Billy's mate,
you battled with management
and mostly won.
You fought with the industry,
at best a score draw.
You fought against stardom
and almost won.
But your own demons
you could never overcome.
'So it's one more drink
you're sailing away'
and 'one drink down
and another to go'.
You stumbled on
with few thoughts of tomorrow,
from Mary Skeffington's child
to reluctant star
with *that* song.
Lost because
you never really found
a home to be dry in.
I hope you sleep well.
Either way,
I hope you've found peace.

17ᵗʰ January 2009

[For Gerry Rafferty 1947 – 2011]

Peering Beyond the Veil

(for Philip K Dick 1928-1982)
From cosmic puppets to transmigrations,
from record shop to Hollywood.

Your writings are not a series of
adventures but rather a journey
from frightened to searching to
madness and then back to searching
for a peace that you never really
found and yet which you were
so sure was there, just on the
Edge of your vision, beyond all
the nightmares and the fears and
whilst you never found the answers
you got pretty good at knowing
the right questions.

You searched the Holy Bible and
the forbidden books, the madness
of the world around you and the
madness that lay within you.

And while you longed for acceptance
you were unwilling to compromise.

O what sublime madnesses are there,
hidden in your books and driven by
the love and compassion that you
strove to communicate to any that

would listen to or read your words.

You peopled your worlds with all the
losers, lovers, lost souls and the
frightened and the damned and the
saved and the wild and the terminally
timid and the demanding, the divine
and the alien that you knew lived in
this world and just beyond it.

From trailer trash prophets to kitchen
sink messiahs and compassionate
policemen, space, time and the edges
of perception, all were in a state of flux
and all possessed the potential for
finding grace within themselves.

Always, somewhere behind the despair
and fatalism that struck down your
characters, there was hope and the
opportunity for wisdom and transcendence,
seldom taken or achieved, sometimes
rejected or misunderstood, but always there,
somewhere in the background or at
the edges of the picture.

And through it all you struggled
and scrimped in a world that was
simply not ready for your visions
or your fragile and frequently fractured
realities and para-realities that may

just have been more real than the
world that we see around us.

But you had to write too much and
it drove you to madness and an act
of almost successful self-destruction

And then what may have been divine
intervention or might just as likely
have been the drugs and the stress
plunging you into the insanity that
lay at the very core of the century
to which you belonged and somehow
transcended using no more than the
sheer force of your vision and the
drive of your fears.

And then, as your book drew to
a close, Hollywood came knocking
and sold a vision stripped of all
your dreams but in the long run
dragged your work into the mainstream
and gave you in death all of the
respect that you were denied in
this mortal coil.

We still see though a darkening
scanner, still have the bomb and
the fear that produced it but
that dim and uncertain beacon
you lit still shines its fragile light

and I'm sure that, if nothing else,
William Blake would have understood.

31ˢᵗ January 2009

For Walt W

I rise up to the new day
sing the joys of life
the blood surging through my
body in a power that is
electric and blue.

27ᵗʰ December, 2007
[for Walter Whitman 1819 – 1892]

A Second Poem for William Blake

Songs from pure ideal
of hope and transcendence
innocence first epitomised then questioned by
songs with darker visions
of pragmatic realism borne of vicarious
experience completing the precarious balance

27ᵗʰ December, 2007

Goodbye, Mr Mitchell

A big heart,
always on the left,
always open,
always true,
always just,
you.

Voice or shadow,
all the light
there is in
this world will
shine a little dimmer.

Sleep well.

You've earned your rest
and fear not.

I will never read
your poetry to
any class with
more than 20
students,
and even then
only if they
really want
to hear it.

One day the world will

be run over by truth.

Until then I will
cling to the dream.

Goodbye, Mr Mitchell

21ˢᵗ December 2008
[For Adrian Mitchell. 24ᵗʰ October 1932 – 20ᵗʰ December 2008]

For JHS

John Heath-Stubbs
will write no more.

A bold bard barking
with your love of sound.

Your little creatures
and your Roman heroes.

Four score years and eight,
chasing the muse
where the flea
showed his heels
to the Pope.

26ᵗʰ December 2006

[for John Heath-Stubbs 1918-2006]

The Violinist

He walks out onto the stage,
violin and bow in hand.
Applause surrounds him
as he approaches the stand.
A dignified bow, then
as he shifts into the playing position
a subtle transformation takes place
as man
and violin
and bow
all merge
and a musician appears
where a few seconds before
was only a man.

19th, October, 2007

Because the Ending

(For The Man in Black)

Deep, slow, broken.

That voice pulls the words
from deep within
'Oh Lord, help me to walk
one more mile, just one more mile'.

It is the voice of age.

The sound of loneliness and
an ending expressed in song.

And at the same time it
is still the man in black,
is still the voice.

And still the faith carries
him onwards,
for though June had gone
still you sang.

But then you were gone too,
as you finally loosed the shackles
that bound you to this coil.

But still your soul
can be heard by
anybody who cares to listen
to a voice that echoes with
gravitas without even trying.

The sound of a solitary man
walking one hundred highways
just to be free from the chain gang.

One more mile.

Just one more mile.

2nd August 2009
[for John R. Cash 1932 - 2003]

On playing Tangerine Dream's 'Zeit' at half speed

Time
stretches.
The music plays on.
Four tracks,
one double album,
but slowed
and thus stretched.
The chords' familiar shapes
seemingly reduced to nothing
and yet still there
giving the sound its shape
and its direction.
Melodic content removed still further
from its traditional role in the centre.
A role here served by texture
and the textural development of chords
as melodies stretched beyond the point
at which the mind perceives them as such
and within the space
all this sound generates
is a peace and a calm
that makes things
that little bit more
worth while.

10th August 2008

Remembering Ian Curtis

You informed us
love would tear us apart,
but we had no idea
you meant to depart.

We played the records.
We lived through the gigs.
We told all who listened
you were going to be big.

You gave form to our shadows.
You lifted the lid on your pain.
You feared for tomorrow,
now we'll never see you again.

Could these sensations make me feel
the pleasures of a normal man?
was too much of a question
to be answered by a mere music fan.
Ashamed of the things we've been put through
we find a way out if we can.

We saw our pain through your words
and hoped for unknown pleasures
but now you have left us
we have only memories to treasure.

Abandoned too soon
you left us without goodbye
the journey we started with you
was not complete when you died.

198

Yes, we are the young men
with a weight on our shoulders.
We cope with the dark and the quiet
and learn to get older.
You left us with 'Closer'
but we're further apart.
We looked for an answer
but now have only your art

Is this the role that you wanted to live?
Could you really not bear to continue?
Why did you so emphatically decide
you simply had no more to give?

So I play your records
and hear your voice
but I hear in the words
you left yourself no choice.

You lived a life in your music,
but believed in what you did.
Your dreams full of darkness
God alone knows where you hid.
Your words and voice
I will remember long but
at the final test
you were not that strong.
You explored your nightmares
only to discover when
faced with your own demons
you were *too frail to wake this time*

Monday, 31 July 2000

Irreverent Response #1

Leafing through a book
of twentieth century Italian art
in the library one day
as I'm sure we all do
from time to time.

A colour plate of Il Cavallo Bianco e Il Molo
painted between 1920 and 1922
by one Mario Sironi
caught my eye
as a strong image can.

The horse strutting down the road
pulling its shadow with it,
rider keeping an eye
on the scenery as
the horse takes him on his way.

All else is lines and texture
in the softening light
of the evening sun.

Just beyond the boundaries
of the painting lies
a world of industry and society
but within the is only
the wall and the road,
and the horse and the man,
both forever caught
at the moment

of departure.

[After *'The White Horse and the Pier'* by *Mario Sironi* (1885-1961)]

8th August 2008

Irreverent Response #2

The powerful jawline and sharp teeth
do little to offset the meekness.
Bowl held warily in both hands
as if in fear that it might burn or bite.
The eyes are open wide in apparent supplication.
Legs awkwardly crossed,
presumably in a desperate attempt
to prevent incontinence.
The figure oozes embarrassment
possibly from being caught in public
wearing those oh-so unfashionable arm bands.

[after an animal figure from Baoule on the Ivory Coast]

8th August 2008

Irreverent Response #3

Lisa Gherardini sits and waits.
Francesco her beloved husband
wanted a portrait and wanted the best.

So here she sits patiently
resting her hands in her lap as

she posed for the talented
bastard son from Florence,
and patient she must be
for Leo is not the quickest of painters.

But she doesn't mind
she just hopes that her expression
doesn't make it too obvious
that she's off her face on grass
and fantasising having sex with Francesco
in the great hall of St. Peter's Basilica
while his holiness gives mass from the balcony.

She's not sure what Leo's been smoking either
because that background he's got planned
is pretty wild and will probably be replaced
by some kind of landscape.

There are worse ways to pass the days.

8ᵗʰ August 2008

*After the Portrait of Lisa Gherardini wife of Francesco del
Giocondo by Leonardo da Vinci.*

For the Countess of Glamis

O, Lady Macbeth
you dreamed
of being queen.
That your noble husband
would rule the big country
wise and long.

But he wasn't
and he didn't.
And all you got
was what you
thought you wanted
rather than
that which
you needed.

13th January, 2007

For Stuart Adamson

You sit there,
utterly alone.
Your time came
but now it has gone,
leaving you
one of yesterday's men.

Even the big country
little remembers you.

Whiskey your only friend.

You take a last breath,
step forward
and fall into
your final bow.....

25th February, 2007

Say it Loud

James Brown has gone
away for good this time
but we can still hear
his sex machine
purring in the corner
and his spirit is still
living in America.

We ain't got you no more
but we can still feel good.

Monday, 25th December, 2006

[for James Joseph Brown (1933-2006)]

On Reading Langston Hughes

I am reading my book of Langston Hughes
Beautiful words that move (and groove)

In seven words he said more
than the likes of me could
say in six pages or more.

I read and then I
see how beautiful
you still are.

Long gone but we
still hang on to

your dreams of rivers.

31ˢᵗ December, 2014
*[for (*James Mercer) Langston Hughes 1902-1967)

Song to Bob

Hey, hey, Bob Dylan
I'm writing this of you
and though the words are shaky
all they say will be true.

You came
armed with no more
than your pen and paper,
a voice, guitar,
a piano & an harmonica,
and a confidence that you
had something to offer.

But who could have guessed
the quiet, shaky voice that sang
'When I Got Troubles'
back in nineteen fifty nine
would bestride the world
and give it no choice
than to listen or to quibble
over your words or your voice
as you wrote, played and sang
about people, minds and time,
not flowers, sunsets or birds
so that now you stand tall

one foot in eternity and the other
between the street and the harbour.

Yearning for the clouds,
for a heart in the highlands.
Ain't talking, still singing and playing
as the world it moves on
and times are a-changing.

We still haven't counted the roads,
have closed our eyes to the wind
If it takes a lot to laugh
then our train can but cry.

I see you're still searching
and only you can say why.

1ˢᵗ December 2008

Thespian

The ageing actor stood in the wings
and awaited his cue that would
prompt him to walk onto the stage
as Friar Laurence and approach
the Capulet's monument in his
failed bid to prevent three deaths.

In his time he had appeared as
Tybolt, Count Paris, Mercutio,
Romeo, Prince Escalus,
Montague, Capulet and

now he was the sweet Friar.

This was his three hundred
and forty seventh time he
had helped bring this play
to life for an eager audience.

He had seen the play through
so many different roles and
still it felt slightly different
each and every time.

His very first performance
as a fully paid up actor
had been shortly after
his sixteenth birthday
as a last minute stand-in
for an indisposed Tybolt.

And now he stood once more
in the wings of a small theatre
awaiting his cue for his final
appearance of the night.

But tonight was much more
to him than merely
the final scene of
an oft acted, tragic play.

Tonight he would play the
well meaning friar for the

first and the last time.
Fifty years almost to the day
from that barely noticed
professional debut,
he would bring to an end
a long sequence of varied
character renditions that,
while appreciated by his
colleagues for their safe
and dependable nature,
never rose above the same
old barely noticed level
for both critics and audiences.

And suddenly, as never before,
a fear gripped him tight and
he could hardly bring himself
to breathe let alone take note
of what was happening on stage.

Not now!
He had never gone up once.
Remembering his lines was
something he did without ever
giving it a second thought.

But tonight, as he made his
predictably unannounced
exit from the world of theatre
(as if anybody would care),
he found his mind a blank.

He knew he was no longer
even the minor actor he
had been before the fall and
that his appearance tonight
owed more to the sympathy
of his colleagues than to
any magic he might bring
to this often elusive part.

He didn't care about the limp,
it was there and he was more
than experienced enough as
an actor to build it into his
performance but this trick
of his memory was nothing
less than cruel and spiteful.

His eyes glazed and he
tilted his face up towards
the rafters and prayed to
his God for the first time
in more years than he cared
to attempt remembering.

He remembered his first
time in a lead role,
predictably as Romeo.
Indeed the play had been
there at every important
point in his long career

as a board treading Thespian.

He remembered meeting
his wife at the first read
through of an earlier run
where he was cast as
Benvolio and she in
her element as Juliet.

Their marriage was the
most wonderful day of
his life and the source
of more of his pain than
everything else put together.

He closed his eyes and
pictured her face as it was
before that terrible day
on the midland motorway.

He could hear her voice
and he almost called out
her name before he stopped,
drew a deep, calming breath,
and took his cue from there.

He strode onto the stage
and declaimed
"Saint Francis be my speed!
How oft to-night?
Have my old feet

stumbled at graves!
Who's there?"

Minutes later he took his bow
and left the theatre for
the very last time and
made his way back home.

8th August, 2017

Alphabetic Index

Printed in Great Britain
by Amazon